Equality and Social Policy

Edited by **WALTER FEINBERG**

Equality and Social Policy

UNIVERSITY OF ILLINOIS PRESS

URBANA CHICAGO LONDON

Publication of this work was aided by a grant
from the National Institute of Education.

Library of Congress Cataloging in Publication Data

Main entry under title:

Equality and social policy.

   Papers of a conference sponsored by the National In-
stitute of Education (Division of Equity) and held at the
University of Illinois, Mar. 9–10, 1976.
   Includes bibliographical references.
   1. Equality—Congresses.   2. Educational equaliza-
tion—Congresses.   3. Civil rights—Congresses.
I. Feinberg, Walter, 1937-   II. National Institute
of Education. Educational Equity Group.
HM146.E65   323.4   77-16431
ISBN 0-252-00215-6

Contents

WALTER FEINBERG

Introduction

The ideal of human equality, as Mihailo Marković points out in this volume, is a prime example of a moral principle the meaning of which has evolved over time. Originally the idea applied only to the spiritual aspect of human life—all "men" were equal because they all possessed human souls—but in time it was applied to legal, political, and economic situations as well. Yet, as Marković also notes, in contemporary liberal society the idea of human equality has been applied to the different spheres of human life in an abstract way and has thereby served to mask certain tensions in the historical manifestation of the idea. People are judged to be equal in contemporary terms if they have been granted, in the economic sphere, equality of opportunity and, in the political sphere, equality of rights. Yet the worth of political rights—the extent to which they can actually be used to exercise uncoerced judgment successfully—is dependent to a large extent upon the material resources that people have available to them, and, unfortunately, the doctrine of equality of opportunity, even when properly applied, is consistent with a large amount of actual inequality.

This tension in the modern notion of equality seems to call for a reinterpretation of the concept, and in the area of social policy there have in fact been a number of challenges to the traditional notion of equality of opportunity. In some instances, social policy has pushed the boundaries of our moral judgment. However, even though these challenges have served to highlight some of the problems with the concept, most of them have accepted the core idea of equality of opportunity—that rewards ought to correspond in

1

a direct way to talent. Once this idea is accepted, of course, then it becomes largely an empirical question whether in fact any given society corresponds to it. The papers in this volume, however, were intended not only to examine this empirical issue, but also to begin to analyze the concept of equality that lies behind it, and to begin to sketch some of the different kinds of policies that can emerge from different interpretations of equality. Before turning to the papers, it will be useful to look at the way in which some of the recent challenges have been limited by an acceptance of the core meaning of equality of opportunity.

Among the most recent and most publicized challenges to dominant views concerning equality of opportunity were the various compensatory programs initiated in the middle 1960s. These included programs such as Head Start on the preschool level, Upward Bound at the high school level, and the Special Education Opportunities Program at the college level. The fact that many of the programs developed at this time were carried out in school is significant, for it reflected the belief that the historical inequities developed in social, political, and economic life could be corrected through an emphasis on education. The challenge, however, was not to equality of opportunity as a guiding social principle, but rather to some of the practices which people felt were in fact inhibiting the expression of this idea. Certainly, it was thought, talent should be rewarded, but it can't be rewarded properly unless it has a true opportunity to express itself. The fact that many of the early programs were directed at black people, a group in which the intensity of discrimination was obvious, made it easier to focus on the level of procedures while ignoring the actual range of inequalities which the social institutions had encouraged.

Once some people began to believe that these compensatory programs were not likely to significantly effect a more equal distribution of rewards across groups, however, they began to respond in a number of different ways. Some, such as Arthur Jensen and others who believe in the validity of IQ scores as a measure of intelligence, attempted to deny the empirical assumption that supported these programs. They argued the old thesis that intellectual capacities varied between racial groups and that these intellectual differences limited the ability of some people to profit from any education that involved more than the rote learning of certain skills. Even though his case was built on questionable evidence, much of which was later challenged, the effect of Jensen's argument was to lend support to those who wished to believe that contemporary social problems were the result not of opportunities denied, but of the natural inability of some to take advantage of opportunities offered.[1] Thus the general thrust of Jensen's work was to reaffirm the traditional notion of equality of opportunity and of America as a society that approximates the ideal.

Another prominent response to the inability of compensatory programs to significantly address discrepancies in the distribution of social rewards and positions was to begin, at least slightly, to shift the focus of equality of opportunity away from individuals and toward groups. Mosteller and Moynihan explain the reasons for this shift in the following way: "Herein lies the fundamental conflict. The Civil Rights Act of 1964 was on the surface the very embodiment of the former tradition. In effect it outlawed group identification. No individual was to be labeled: not by race, religion, national origin, nor even for certain purposes by sex. Yet the act arose largely out of concern for the status of a special group: the Negro. Inevitably its enactment and administrative interpretation led to the formal assertion of group rights and interest by the national government."[2] To a certain extent this explanation is accurate, for it was out of a concern for groups that such policies as affirmative action were initiated. However, what Mosteller and Moynihan fail to recognize is that the concept of a group and its well-being was used in an ambiguous way and was often artificially grafted on to the older concept of equality of opportunity as applied to individuals. The failure to address this initial ambiguity can in fact account for many of the successful challenges to affirmative action programs today, and we can better understand this ambiguity by looking at two different kinds of justifications for affirmative action programs.

The first of these justifications, and the one which is the more common, looks at equality of opportunity as largely a procedural matter, the idea of which is to eliminate any discriminatory practices in the selection of individuals to certain positions. Thus the fact that any particular group is underrepresented in a particular area serves as prima facie evidence that the procedures may in fact be discriminatory and provides reason for checking those procedures. The strength of this justification for rectifying inequality on the distributive level then depends largely upon how liberally the notion of a procedure is interpreted. For example, a medical school program that views the public school opportunities of different groups as a factor in the question of fair competition is likely to have a more sustained impact on the number of black physicians than one that simply looks at the racial bias that may be contained in certain admissions tests. Yet this way of looking at affirmative action, while seeming to make equality of opportunity a function of groups, in reality reinforces the idea that it is mainly a function of individuals. The distribution of positions across groups serves *only* as a prima facie reason to suspect that there may be inequalities in the procedures for selecting individuals.[3]

The second justification, one that is less prominent than the first and often only implicit in certain arguments,[4] judges social progress in terms of how status and positions are distributed among individuals in one group as compared to individuals in another. The more closely the range of distribution found among members of a minority group approximates that to be found among members of a dominant group, the greater is judged to be the progress. Thus in this case an uneven distribution between groups is not taken simply as prima facie evidence for examining the fairness of procedures. Rather, it is the primary measure of social justice and fairness. In this justification the group is more truly the focus of equal opportunity than in the former one. However, what is also important to understand is that here the group functions largely as a statistical norm and that just below the surface of the newer interpretation is the older one which still views equality of opportunity as a function of individuals. Given the way in which these two interpretations function together, this latter justification then becomes quite consistent with a great deal of actual discrimination between groups. For example, one of the most forceful justifications for affirmative action programs is that they will provide depressed groups with the trained personnel needed to improve the quality of life for all. Thus, for example, it is argued that by training more doctors from minority groups, who will then work in the ghettos and depressed areas of this country, the health of the entire community will be improved. Yet given the *ad hoc* way in which individual and group rights are fused together, the very strength of this argument rests upon a discriminatory assumption. As one physician has pointed out: "Black (medical) students have another problem. They are the objects of another subtle form of racism. Many institutions are willing to train black students for the ghetto but other students are expected to enjoy a free choice."[5] What this remark indicates is that two different interpretations of equality of opportunity, when applied simultaneously, can function to discriminate against minority group members. When applied to dominant groups, equality of opportunity is applied to individuals who are then given a free choice as to what to do with those opportunities. For members of minorities, however, the choice is restricted. Given this discrepancy and given, too, the way in which medical students are selected, socialized, and trained, it becomes uncertain whether black students will in fact allow themselves to be deprived of certain individual rights in order to improve the health of their community.[6]

If, however, we attempt to remove these discriminatory assumptions and simply measure the progress of society on the basis of how closely the distribution of status and rewards within one group approximates the distribution to be found within another group, then the idea of equality of opportunity as applied to groups becomes consistent with a great deal of inequality *within* different groups. In other words, if we are concerned only with the distribution across groups, then the question still remains as to how opportunities are to be distributed within groups. And since the dominant group serves here as the model in allocating rewards as a function of individuals, then whatever level of inequality is found in that group likely becomes the level that is viewed as tolerable for the minority group as well. Moreover, assuming that the allocation of rewards within the dominant group is justified as conforming to the concept of equality of opportunity as applied to individuals, then it becomes problematic why the application of this concept *across* groups should be justified as anything but a historically contingent correction procedure. For if equality of opportunity as applied to individuals is seen to be a reasonable procedure for allocating rewards within groups, then why, it may be asked, should it not also be seen as a reasonable method for applying rewards and status across groups as well. It is of course possible to respond to this challenge to equality of opportunity as applied to groups by arguing that past discriminatory practices have retarded minority group members from achieving rewards commensurate with their talents. This response, while historically sound, has the disadvantage of interpreting the application of the principle to groups as only an intermediate and corrective measure, one which should be done away with as soon as the conditions are established which allow members of minority groups to express their "true talents." Furthermore, given the assumption that talent is in fact distributed equally among groups, then this application of equality of opportunity, while consistent with a highly integrated class structure at all levels, is also consistent with a large degree of inequality between the different classes.

While it is unlikely that the general public will articulate these conceptual relationships fully, the failure of recent policy to address a systematic challenge to the concept of equal opportunity as applied to individuals has left much of the traditional moral sensitivities intact and acts as a pressure against any far-reaching approach to social policy. And, given Marković's observations about the real connection between economic well-being and political equality, the failure to provide a systematic challenge can only serve to mask the real inequalities which continue to exist in contemporary liberal society. Marković's and the other essays in this volume were designed to address some of the dilemmas that arise out of the prevailing interpretation of equality and to provide some of the insights needed to help us think about alternatives. To see how these different essays fit together in a single conference volume, it will be helpful to move beyond the present debate about equality and social policy and to look at the issues in a slightly different context.

6

One of the reasons often given for an interpretation of equality as equality of opportunity is that it is believed to be consistent with a large degree of political freedom. In other words, the government's job is merely to regulate the competition and to then step aside, presumably to allow people to express their rights and run their lives as they will. Whether in fact equality of opportunity actually exists to a reasonable degree in any contemporary society is, of course, an empirical question which needs to be addressed not only in terms of mobility patterns, but also in terms of the material and technological restraints which help us to decide what might be a reasonable degree of mobility for any given society to strive for at a given time. However, the assumption that equality of opportunity is consistent with a minimal state and that a minimal state is consistent with political freedom is more than just a conceptual issue. The extent to which state intervention is justified under this notion of equality depends upon a number of factors, among them the degree of intervention needed to restore and maintain fair competition. Given some situations, as Virginia Held observes in this volume, a commitment to equality of opportunity is quite consistent with a great deal of state intervention. What is clear about this doctrine, as both Held and Marković point out, is that it provides a great advantage to any individual who is able to seize an opportunity and translate it into material resources. Because these advantages relate to political liberties, they influence the worth that such liberties have for any individual.[7] Because there are no limits placed on the amount of material rewards that a person can accumulate, the contemporary interpretation of equality is consistent with a very large amount of political and economic inequality.

As it is presently interpreted, the established image of equality both masks and justifies the level of prevailing inequalities. It does this by singling out as important certain things—such as abstract political rights and economic opportunities—and by de-emphasizing other things as unimportant, such as the large discrepancies in material well-being that are to be found in contemporary society. Yet the fact that these different aspects of equality can be conceived as isolated from each other is at least partly the result of

7

our having forgotten the original context in which these rights were discussed, and it is also partly the result of not taking seriously new factors in the political, social, and economic context in which discussions of them are conducted. We can see this most clearly by focusing on the issue of political rights.

As presently accepted and indeed as originally interpreted, the political rights which people were to possess equally were conceived as residing in individuals. Thus the right to free speech, freedom of assembly, the right to a trial by jury were thought to be rights which individuals had and which they could claim against the state. These rights rested upon a concept of a person as free and independent, and upon a concept of state power as being a grant from the people. However, there is also a difference in the way these rights were originally conceived and the way they are presently interpreted. While they were thought to belong to individuals, they were also justified as among the conditions required for the establishment and maintenance of a public. In other words, if the power of the state was a grant from the people, then the conditions needed to be maintained whereby the people could establish and affect its will. The rights that were acknowledged were done so on this basis. This consideration was not only persuasive when it came to the rights which are *most obviously* required for the maintenance of a public, such as freedom of speech, assembly, and the press, but also for some of the less obvious ones. Thus, an early commentator looked at even the right to a trial by jury from the point of view of its value in maintaining an informed public: "The trial by jury . . . and the collection of the people by their representatives in the legislature, are those fortunate inventions which have procured for them, in this country, their true proportion of influence, and the wisest and most fit means of protecting themselves in the community. Their situation as jurors and representatives, enables them to acquire information and knowledge in the affairs and government of the society; and to come forward, in turn, as the sentinels and guardians of each other."[8]

While it would be clearly a mistake to romanticize the percentage of the population that comprised any kind of a public in revolutionary times, for surely it was small, it is important to recognize that discussions of political rights were carried on in the context of discussions of establishing an active, participating public. (The fact that today the public is more often than not perceived as the passive recipient of policies initiated and administered in governmental bureaus is an indication of how radically these two concepts have been severed from one another.) While freedom of speech, of assembly, and of the press were certainly rights that belonged to individuals, they also belonged to them as members of an actual or potential public that was able to debate issues and develop the critical skills necessary to pass judgment upon governmental and other decisions. Moreover, these rights were thought to be the ingredients that were required to allow the people to establish the normative base which could serve as a check on the authority of special interests. This relationship has been recognized whenever commentators have lamented the loss of the public. What they have lamented has not usually been the loss of abstract political rights, although they have certainly felt these were important to guard, but rather the loss of a set of arrangements, both institutional and cultural, which encouraged people to become active agents in decisions which would affect them all. To the extent that such arrangements were ever reasonably present, then the recognition of abstract, political rights was but a way to maintain and protect them, because these rights guarded essential spheres of expression within which the government was not to interfere.

Whether or not such a public ever existed in this country and, if so, to what extent, is a historical question, but it is important to understand that some of the most fruitful discussions of the nature of these rights were carried on in the context of a concern about the kinds of conditions that would be required for establishing and maintaining a coherent, articulate public which could pass judgment on the activities of government and special interest groups. Once such rights became decontextualized from this other concern, and then were transformed into a society which possessed the techniques for manipulation and control on a massive scale, they were no longer likely to serve as a way to check the excess influence of special interests. Given this transformation, it then becomes a major social question as to how those rights can be reinterpreted and recontextualized so that such a public can emerge.

The concept of the public and its relationship to human rights—both political and economic—is an implicit theme which ties this collection together. Beginning with Orlando Patterson's critique of the equal opportunity doctrine we have an analysis of the economic conditions which serve to keep some people politically isolated and socially alienated. Patterson reminds us that economic growth has not produced economic equality and that prevailing economic policies have been willing to tolerate a large number of people living on the fringes of political and economic life. His paper challenges the assumptions of both conservative and liberal theory as they are used to justify existing inequalities, and it suggests a distribution policy that is intended to more adequately meet the problems generated by inequalities of wealth.

While the concept of the public remains only implicit in Patterson's treatment of the prevailing political and economic inequalities, it is a more central concern in James D. Anderson's treatment of cultural inequities. Anderson's analysis is largely an attempt to understand the ways in which existing ethnic and racial groups could be used as the basis for the formation of a pluralistic public in the United States. He begins by criticizing the idea that cultural equality has been established when members of minority groups have been given an "equal chance" to "participate" in the dominant culture, and he concludes by elaborating some of the prerequisites for a truly pluralistic society.

While Patterson and Anderson provide, from different perspectives, a critique of the idea of equality of opportunity as presently interpreted, Held and Marković add to this a critique of the dominant interpretations of political equality. Both show how the dominant definition of political rights, when coupled with the prevailing interpretation of equality of opportunity, serves to inhibit effective social action. In addition, speaking from his own Yugoslav experience, Marković suggests some of the steps that are required to establish and maintain an effective public.

10

Virginia Held begins the discussion of political rights by critically examining the concept of negative freedom as it has been articulated from Hobbes through Nozick, and she demonstrates the inadequacy of a concept which would grant equal rights without granting effective means. She also shows how the negative interpretation of political "freedom" can be used to drastically restrict real individual liberty. Mihailo Marković's essay describes how the concept of negative freedom arose out of an intellectual tradition which insisted upon splitting society into two conceptually separate spheres —the political and the economic. Once this split was accomplished (at least in thought), then the question of equality could be treated as simply a formal matter. In the political sphere equality became equality before the law, while in the economic sphere equality was translated into equality of opportunity. Marković then points out that once this separation was established it provided a ready excuse for giving little attention to the fact of unequal material conditions under which "some individuals are able to fully enjoy their civil rights, whereas for others most of these rights remain abstract possibilities entirely out of practical reach." Later on in the essay, and drawing from his Yugolsav experience, Marković suggests ways in which a society can pursue the goals associated with human equality without an overemphasis on centralized, bureaucratic modes of decision making. This issue is crucial to any discussion about the establishment and maintenance of an effective public.

Turning from a critique of the concept of equality, the papers of Hu Chang-Tu, Wayne A. O'Neil, and Ronald R. Edmonds examine the actual and possible responses of different institutions to the problems created by inequality. Professor Hu's description of Chinese education since the revolution documents the steps that were taken in that country to reduce the distance between different levels of the society and to establish a spirit of self-reliance among the people. What the Chinese experience suggests is that when educational selection takes place independently of the activities and will of the public, then the educated elite are likely to begin to develop a set of attitudes, concerns, and sensibilities that are in fundamental conflict with those of working people. Hu's outline of the recent history of Chinese education documents the steps that were taken in that country to reduce this tendency.

Wayne O'Neil's paper addresses the possibilities for education in the United States. Drawing upon his own experience of teaching linguistics to ghetto children, O'Neil suggests ways in which education could serve a liberating function in societies such as our own which have the wealth and technology to easily satisfy the basic needs of physical existence. O'Neil's essay is significant for this volume in a number of different ways. First, he draws his analysis from work with groups which fit Patterson's description of being on the margin of contemporary society. In so doing, O'Neil adds to Patterson's critique of the equal opportunity doctrine by countering many of the myths about the ability of such children to learn complicated material. Second, O'Neil highlights an important pedagogical distinction which educators have largely ignored. In teaching complicated linguistics, O'Neil notes, he is drawing on data which are internal rather than external to the children themselves. That is, the material to be analyzed and understood is as familiar to them as their own speech patterns. Finally, O'Neil addresses the very important question of whether a stress on theoretical subjects need be inconsistent with the quest for human equality, and finds that it need not be.

One of the points that is implicit in O'Neil's paper is that the possibilities for the formation of a coherent public at this time in American history may be greater at the fringes of society than at the center. This message is consistent with Anderson's earlier argument that black cultural identity could serve as a model for American pluralism. In many respects, Edmonds's treatment of the delivery of social services is an extension of this theme and a program for its practical implementation in certain areas. He suggests some of the steps which can be taken to give communities more control over economic and social resources and to make social agencies accountable to the communities which they serve.

Finally, Jerry Hirsch and Noam Chomsky provide a catalog of the scientific and nonscientific considerations which need to be kept in mind when deliberating about social organization, and both warn against various attempts to argue for a specific form of social organization on the basis of empirical evidence alone. Hirsch begins by documenting the simple fact of genetic diversity and by reminding us that one of the characteristics of an increasingly humane society is its ability to transcend the struggle for existence found among lower forms of animal life and to accommodate the diverse characteristics of members of the human species. Hirsch then turns his attention to the latest attempt to reduce human life to the simple rules of animal society—E. O. Wilson's *Sociobiology*. Noam Chomsky begins by raising some neglected questions about the relationship between equality and efficiency and equality and freedom, and he questions the view that holds that capitalist institutions promote both freedom and efficiency. While his essay challenges a number of the conceptual and empirical points that are often used to support a large amount of material and political inequality, it also reminds us that a truly just and decent society need not ignore the fact that human beings are different in many important ways.

Any fundamental and systematic examination of human values needs to begin by recognizing where the tensions presently exist and where the reconciliations need to be made. It is, as Chomsky points out, commonly assumed that there is an irreconcilable tension between the value of human equality and the value of individual freedom. Just why we accept this as *the* central conflict in a world where the freedom of some can easily result in the control and manipulation of the many is not obvious and clear. Indeed, given the ever-expanding possibilities for mass manipulation, a greater tension would seem to exist between a notion of equality of opportunity which, even if properly adhered to, is able to justify vast differences in material resources and well-being and a notion of equal political rights which is predicated on the assumption that every individual, through rational reflection and dialogue, is able to reach an uncompelled judgment. Taken as a whole, the essays in this volume are intended to challenge the prevailing assumptions, both factual and conceptual, about the nature of human equality and the policies that issue from accepted interpretations of it.

The papers in this volume were selected from those presented at a conference, The Promise and Problems of Human Equality, held at the University of Illinois on March 9-10, 1976. The conference was sponsored by the National Institute of Education (Division of

Equity) and the following divisions of the University of Illinois at Urbana-Champaign: African Studies Program, Center for Asian Studies, Afro-American Cultural Program, College of Education, Conferences and Institutes division of the Office of Continuing Education, Department of Educational Policy Studies, and Russian and East European Center.

Special appreciation is due to Jerry Hirsch and Brandt Pryor for their help in planning and arranging the conference, to Ray Rist and the National Institute of Education for financial support, and to Ernest Kahane, Stephen Norris, and Chrystal Smith for their editorial assistance.

REFERENCES

1. For a detailed critique of the research and evidence used in the Jensen paper, see Jerry Hirsch, "Jensenism: The Bankruptcy of 'Science' without Scholarship," *Educational Theory,* vol. 25, no. 1 (Winter, 1975), pp. 3-27. For an analysis of some of the conceptual problems in Jensen's and similar positions, see N. J. Block and Gerald Dworkin, "IQ: Heritability and Inequality," *Philosophy and Public Affairs,* parts 1, 2, Summer and Fall, 1974. For a further critique of the implication that Jensen draws for pedagogy see Walter Feinberg, "The Economic and Political Limits to the Humanizing of Education," in Richard H. Weller, ed., *Humanistic Education* (Berkeley, Calif.: McCutchan, 1977).

2. Frederick Mosteller and Daniel P. Moynihan, eds., *On Equality of Educational Opportunity* (New York: Vintage Books, 1972), p. 7.

3. I am indebted to James Anderson for clarifying some points on the operation of affirmative action programs for me.

4. See, for example, Colin Greer's *The Great School Legend* (New York: Basic Books, 1972) for an example of the way this second notion has been used as an implicit guide to arguments about the fairness of American society. For an analysis of this and other literature of its kind see Walter Feinberg, "Revisionist Scholarship and the Problem of Historical Context," *Teachers College Record,* vol. 78, no. 3 (Feb., 1977).

5. M. Alfred Haynes, "Problems Facing the Negro in Medicine Today," *Journal of the American Medical Association,* vol. 209, no. 7 (Aug. 18, 1969).

6. For a more extended treatment of this subject see Walter Feinberg, "An Inquiry into the Growth and Distribution of Medical Knowledge," in Vince Crockerberg and Richard LaBreeque, eds., *Culture as Education,* (Dubuque, Iowa: Kendall/Hunt, 1977).

7. The term "worth of liberty" is borrowed from John Rawl's *Theory of Justice* (Cambridge: Harvard University Press, 1971).

8. "Letters by Richard Henry Lee" in *Federalist and Other Constitutional Papers,* ed. E. H. Scott (Chicago: Albert, Scott & Co., 1896), p. 872.

14

ORLANDO PATTERSON

Inequality, Freedom, and the Equal Opportunity Doctrine

"Modern society," writes Raymond Aron in a recent work, "seems to conform to two imperatives: to produce as much as possible through mastery of the forces of nature and to treat its members as equals. In their relations with their environment, men gravitate toward collective power; in their relations with each other, they proclaim their determination to recognize each other as equal in worth."[1] It is Aron's view that there is some tension between the two imperatives and, in addition, certain contradictions between different egalitarian ideals. On the whole, however, he remains fairly optimistic about the capacity of modern industrial society to resolve these tensions without breaking into disorder.

I do not share his optimism. This is so not because I hold any romantic pseudo-revolutionary views about the imminent collapse of western industrial societies, for such views, I agree with Aron, are now anachronistic. Rather, I am alarmed at a strange and disturbing trend which several observers have detected in modern industrial society. As these societies have become more and more industrialized, there has been a tendency for a larger and larger proportion of the population to become middle or upper-middle class. Indeed, in most of these societies the majority of people are now middle class or better. The majority, in short, share the enormous affluence generated by these societies. However, running along with this trend has been another one which, until recently, has been hidden by the spectacular growth of affluence and the bourgeoisie.

15

This has been the growth of a substantial minority of poor people, some of them desperately poor, in the midst of industrial affluence.[2]

This odd structural development in many western societies has a psychological dimension. There has been a growing hardening of the attitude of the affluent classes toward the poor. Ironically, it would seem that the very existence of abundance and a large group of affluent people is taken by the latter as proof that anyone with a little determination and moral fiber can make it in a western society. The irony, of course, is that the bourgeois conservative who asserts this is perfectly correct. Anyone can make it in modern industrial society, and there are literally hundreds of thousands of cases of individuals from humble backgrounds and with only the minimum of education who have "made it big." But while anyone can make it, not everyone can. There are systemic limits on the total number of openings available. These limits are such that they include the majority of persons in the society, but there are limits. Western society, especially American society, has reached the stage where all but a tiny minority of people have an equal chance of getting a piece of the national pie and where a majority do end up getting not just a part of the pie, but all of it. And herein lies the iniquity. For we have here a race in which the majority of runners are winners and in which the winners take all. This is the realization of one of the worst fears of democracy—the tyranny of the majority.

In this paper I wish to explore the problem of equality in western societies with special reference to the United States. I shall examine the various attempts to come to terms with the egalitarian ideal and the inegalitarian reality of American society, concluding with a critique of what I shall call the equal opportunity doctrine. Finally, I shall attempt to show that it will be in the best interest of the bourgeoisie and the ruling classes to adopt a more egalitarian policy with respect to the minority of poor persons in their societies, since the alternative will be to suffer what will be called the counter-leviathan power of the poor.

When we say that two things are equal we mean that they share common properties. In relations between human beings we deal with social actors—persons—and their interactions, meaning by the latter the treatment of one person by another. In human relationships, then, the idea of equality has to bring together the nature of the relationship and the quality of the actors. In general, equality has been taken to mean similar treatment of actors sharing a given property with respect to that property.

The "same treatment for similar persons" was how Aristotle defined it, but this was somewhat confusing, for no one was more aware of the fact that no two persons were alike. What Aristotle went on to point out was that two persons may be treated alike with respect to some quality, but differently in most other respects. For Aristotle, the concept of equality was central to his theory of justice, and because justice was as much the unequal treatment of unequals as it was the equal treatment of equals, the Aristotelian theory of justice was quite consistent with a highly unequal social order.[3]

Clearly, the first problem facing ethical theorists concerned with the problem of equality is the empirical fact that persons differ in both individual and group properties—i.e., in terms of qualities such as age, sex, race, cognitive skills, physical prowess, and the like. Some of these differences we disregard, others we consider important, and still others we consider important at one time, then change our minds about and consign to the category of the unimportant. On what basis are these decisions made? What determines the criteria of relevance in our selection of properties? My own view, which coincides with that of a substantial number of ethical theorists, is that all criteria of relevance are value judgments.

Some theorists have attempted to get around this problem by concentrating on so-called objective qualities—e.g., IQ or years of schooling—claiming that persons with unequal quantities of these qualities should be treated differently. But the concentration on measurable qualities—assuming for the moment that one finds such measurements acceptable—merely begs the question. We still need to know why IQ or years of schooling should be selected as relevant. It was partly to answer this question that one of the most durable, although fallacious, attempts to determine criteria of relevance was developed. This is the functionalist argument, first made famous by Davis and Moore.[4] The thesis, quite simply, is that society needs for its survival certain skills, that occupations may be ranked on a hierarchy of structural significance, and that the unequal distribution of income and status insures that the high-level, low-supply skills are provided. Inequality of income is a function of the unequal structural significance of occupations. One may rephrase the argument in Aristotelian terms as follows: equal pay for equal functional significance; unequal pay for unequal functional significance.

The problem with this theory is that no sociologist has ever come up with a persuasive statement concerning the intrinsic relative functional value of occupations. Thus, for example, the high rewards doctors receive for their work may be due to their relative scarcity, but the shortage of doctors is largely an artificially created problem, the combined impact of a rapacious medical profession and a thoroughly heartless government medical policy. The shortage has little or nothing to do with the intellectual demands on medical students. There are thousands of young Americans driving taxis or working as clerks who possess both the intelligence and the motivation to become doctors should the artificial restraints imposed by the shortage of medical schools be removed.

Furthermore, the functionalist argument cannot explain why it is that an actor playing a doctor on T.V. gets maybe ten times more income than the real doctor he plays or why in the midst of an energy crisis a truck driver or a Playboy bunny gets a higher annual starting income than a university physicist working on energy problems. The sad truth is that the income individuals receive is a reflection of the laws of demand and supply, but these laws are in no way a reflection of the intrinsic social worth of occupations. They reflect, rather, the whims of an imperfect free market system and the manipulations of demand by producers and advertising agencies.

Functionalist attempts to define criteria of relevance are, in fact, both teleological and tendentious. Occupations are presumed to be important because they serve the purpose of a given social order. But what makes the purpose of a given social order a valid basis for the determination of relevant criteria? What is sacred about maintaining a given social order? Why should stability determine the criteria of relevance?

Not only is the functionalist attempt to define objective criteria of relevance hopelessly confused, it is also partly irrelevant. It deals only with presumed actual differences and leaves untouched that whole category of qualities which are unquestionably normative —for example the libertarian values of free speech, the right to vote, equality before the law, and the like. Our decision to treat these qualities as among those held equally by all persons is completely valuational.

The concern with criteria of relevance comes about only if we assume that there are real differences among individuals and that these differences are not superficial but are profoundly meaningful in their nature and significance. There are, however, two other positions which one may take as a starting point in approaching the problem of equality. One is to admit that differences exist, but that these are largely environmentally determined and are therefore changeable. The other is to adopt the view that all human differences are trivial and that the differences in emphasis which we place on the superficial qualities that account for the apparent differences are entirely determined by our prejudices. No one, apart from some anarchists, holds the latter position in its extreme form. Even so, it should be noted that this extreme position is not so irresponsible as it may appear at first sight. As a true humanist, one could very reasonably take the view that the qualities on which human beings differ constitute such a tiny fraction of their total number of qualities, the vast majority of which they share, that an emphasis on the differences is at best a necessary evil and at worst a form of human perversity. This, at any rate, tends to be the drift of my thoughts whenever I reflect upon those academic lepers who scamper around the country preaching their doctrine of racial inequality.

Most radical egalitarians have adopted the position that there are certain basic respects in which human beings must be treated either as equal or in a manner tending toward greater equality. Among the rights involved are the right to vote and to participate in the government of one's society, the right to a certain minimum level of literacy, and, for some the most important, the right to an equal share in the wealth and income of one's country.

At this point we approach the present state of the debate on equality in the United States. Most liberals and a good many conservatives are in general agreement on the necessity for an expansion of the number of ways in which people should be treated as equal. Two basic problems remain, however. One is the degree of egalitarianism to be allowed with respect to the distribution of rewards; the other is the means of attaining this degree of egalitarianism.

Both these problems have a factual and an ethical component and we will examine them briefly with respect to the most crucial right under dispute: material security. Even the most conservative members of the more advanced industrial countries agree that certain minimum standards of subsistence must be established, and they are prepared to place a floor of material security below which no one should fall. Thus what is meant by material security is equality in the distribution of the right to a minimum standard of living. What is not meant, and what is rejected as unjust, is the competing view that there should be a gradual narrowing of the gap between the rich and the poor, that, in other words, there should be more equal distribution of material rewards, tending toward, though not necessarily ever attaining, the limit of complete equality. This is viewed with horror by the basic-needs group, who further bolster their opposition to any limitless narrowing of the gap by arguing that such a development would reduce the motivation to work and would be wrong, if not downright sinful, in rewarding sloth and laziness, these being, of course, the prime causes of poverty in the eyes of the prosperous.

It is interesting to observe how closely the moral and factual arguments cohere on both sides of this debate. In general, the conservative basic-needs-and-no-more advocates adopt an absolutist approach to poverty, viewing it as a fixed economic base which may only change to take account of inflation. The other, liberal, side argues for a relativist approach to poverty, asserting, as Lee Rainwater has done in recent works,[5] that basic needs change and are a function of people's perceptions of their relative status, that there is no such thing as an absolute poverty line, this being nothing more than a figure arbitrarily plucked out of the head of some bureaucrat, and that there are conceptions of minimum levels of living and decency shared by all members of the society.

Now it is obvious that any attempt to redistribute income involves the use of inegalitarian means, or rules of allocation, for the attainment of egalitarian ends. The conservative absolutists are prepared to put up with such inequality in the allocatory rules only insofar as it insures minimum standards. Beyond this point the use of such inegalitarian rules of allocation is considered unjust. Liberals agree that the allocatory rules are inegalitarian, but insist that the criterion of justice should be the end result of a rule. Thus transfer payments are just because of the equalization of income they bring about.

A radical critic may point out that both the liberals and the conservatives accept in principle the necessity for a social hierarchy and that both accept the need for some redistribution of income. They differ mainly in the degree of redistribution they would like to bring about. Both are in agreement in rejecting even the preliminary Marxist ethic, "to each according to his needs, from each according to his ability," a position which is quite consistent with a capitalist welfare state.

Why do the liberals hold back? Why do they join ranks with the conservatives in rejecting the view that each should be provided according to his needs? Because of their fear that to push the egalitarian ethic too far might result in conflicts with other strongly held ideals. Later we shall consider these conflicts. Before doing so, however, let us consider the problem of the means of attaining greater equality. We have seen that the liberals are as uncomfortable as the conservatives with the use of direct means of income transfer. Partly this is due to moral scruples and their commitment to rights of property, but partly it is due to the view, which liberals and conservatives alike share, that poverty is due to certain deformities in the character of the poor.

Liberals, and not a few conservatives, have solved the problem of direct income transfer, and of the potential conflict between such direct redistribution with libertarian values, by an appeal to the equal opportunity doctrine. According to this doctrine, everyone should be given an equal chance to compete for the national cake. The institution which will bring this about is education. By insuring that everyone has an equal chance to develop to the fullest extent of his abilities, and by eliminating privilege in access to all openings, inequality and injustice will be abolished.

Let us first examine closely what the equal opportunity doctrine asserts and, more important, what it does not assert. The doctrine assumes that competition will continue and, indeed, is good for society. No moral arguments are offered for its intrinsic goodness —at least I have never read an attempt to justify competition as a virtue in itself—rather, it is justified on utilitarian grounds. It is claimed that competition best insures that the most qualified and competent persons are selected for the jobs, especially the most demanding jobs, in the society. And what about the remainder, those less intellectually gifted and less obsessively competitive types? Liberals are generally vague and often a little sheepish about this group, but if pushed on the issue they will admit that the mass of the less competent will be relegated to inferior roles and status. We are here back to the old meritocracy argument, which is itself merely a special version of the functionalist theory discussed and dismissed earlier. We might only add that the meritocratic version of the functionalist defense of inequality is the most tendentious of all. It is no accident that the only persons who have ever taken it seriously are academics, the only segment of the society to which the argument has some relevance. It is truly amazing how adept human beings are at projecting their own experiences on the rest of the world. Now I have never met Henry Ford II, but I am positive that I can say at least three things about him with a fair degree of certainty. One is that he has never read Herrnstein or Jensen. The second is that if he read them he would not understand them. And the third is that if he understood them he would immediately reject them. There is that delightfully vulgar American rhetorical question, If you're so smart how come you're not rich? I would like to turn this question around and, like an intellectual rotten tomato, throw it at both meritocrats and plutocrats, to wit, If they're so rich, how come they aren't smart?

Second, it should be emphasized that the equal opportunity doctrine is in no way intended to change the structure of inequality in society: it merely seeks to increase the circulation up and down the ladder of success or failure. Furthermore, if we accept the Herrnstein-Jensen-Shockley argument concerning the heritability of intelligence and if it is assumed that equal opportunity will lead to a growing correlation between intelligence and achievement, it will be seen that within a few generations there will emerge the most rigid form of hierarchy ever devised by man, so rigid that even the Indian caste system would seem like a liberal dream in comparison. The different classes will then achieve their different statuses purely on the basis of heredity, only now the heredity of genes rather than wealth. Stratification among human beings will have soared to the biological perfection of the social insects. Since that day is yet to come, and since most liberals have, with a good deal of embarrassment, recoiled from the racist reduction of their argument, we will not pursue the biological arguments any further.

Instead, we will assume that all liberals are the good environmentalists they claim to be. Even so, where does that get us with respect to an improvement in equality through equal opportunity? The answer is nowhere. Absolutely nowhere. The main reason for the failure of the equal opportunity doctrine is the fact that it takes no account of the structure of inequality in society. However, a good part of its failure must also be attributed to its excessive emphasis on the role of education as a means of solving all the problems of the modern world. Liberals, with a doggedness that can only be described as perverse, refuse to recognize the fact that the educational institution is not and cannot be an agent of social change, that it invariably reflects the society in which it exists, its main role being to pass on traditional values and skills and to certify those who, for reasons having little to do with their education, are destined to be successful.

Americans, however, persist in making two claims for education, neither of which has any basis in fact. One is the claim that it will change the structure of the social order and create a more egalitarian society, and the second is that it will make for greater openness in the mobility of individuals. There is no evidence whatever that education does the first. Indeed, there is reason to believe that it does quite the opposite, by reinforcing preexisting status differences. And there is much moral confusion on the issue. Let us assume that there are two individuals of equal intelligence, A, who is upper class, and B, who is lower class. At age six they start with zero units of education and at age eighteen they each have twelve units of education. Obviously, nothing has changed with respect to their relative statuses, even though they have had equal educational opportunities. Indeed, since A begins his education with superior socioeconomic advantages, it is highly likely that A's twelve units of education, even if gained from the same school as B's, are qualitatively superior to B's in that his more favorable home environment has enabled him or her to maximize the inputs of his educational experience.

But let us not stop here. Suppose that by some breakthrough in remedial training we were able to compensate B's inferior environmental background and suppose, further, that we decided to penalize A for his upper-class background by giving him only ten year-units of education while we give B fourteen year-units. Would this make a difference in either the structure of inequality in the society or the relative life chances of A and B? Again the answer is no in both cases.

If one wants to demonstrate how poor a tool the educational institution is as an agent of social change, one merely has to take a look at the experience of developing countries, where each year vast amounts of hard-earned national income are spent under the mistaken belief that by educating the masses economic development will somehow miraculously come about.[6] Now there can be no doubt that for a country with zero, or near zero, literacy education is a vital necessity. In such desperately backward countries, too, it is usually the case that the supply of jobs, mainly in the expanding government sector, is greater than the pool of qualified workers. Most developing countries, however, have long passed this point. In so doing they have come to discover a most disconcerting fact, namely, that once basic literacy has been achieved the returns on educational investment begin to diminish rapidly and, beyond a certain point, the returns indeed become negative. This is so because the rate of educational output tends to outpace, at a geometric rate, the rate of output of new jobs. Once a person is educated beyond a certain level, however, he will not accept certain kinds of jobs. The result is the familiar syndrome in many middle- and upper-range developing countries—high levels of unemployment going along with pockets of rural labor shortage. All that the educational system has done in these upper-level developing countries has been to prepare and certify a small minority of the masses for the elite positions created by the removal of the colonial elite and the expansion of the governmental machinery as well as the light industrial sector. Once these jobs are filled the main role of the educational institution has been to generate people with expectations which cannot be met.[7]

But to get back to the liberal defense of the equal opportunity doctrine. While it might be conceded that education has done nothing to change the structure of inequality in America, it could still be claimed that education deserves some credit for creating a more fluid pattern of mobility. The system may be unequal, but everyone now has an even chance of succeeding. On closer examination even this argument turns out to be utterly without foundation either on moral or empirical grounds. First, let us return to our hypothetical characters A and B mentioned earlier. Morally, it can be argued that since A and B had equal intelligence and since A was deprived in order to bring B up to par with him, it would be unjust if B was further rewarded with higher status, since the two are now equal and there is no reason why the Aristotelian rule of equal shares to equals should not apply. Thus even if the liberal environmentalist were to achieve his dream of a population which, through equal educational opportunity, achieved equal excellence on the part of all its members, the liberal would find an impossible situation in which equals were treated unequally in view of the persisting unequal structure of the society and the incapacity of the educational institution to change it. One can now understand why it is that all liberals, sooner or later, return to the meritocracy thesis, in spite of the ease with which it lends itself to racist sympathizers. The inability of the educational institution to change the structure of inequality leaves the liberal with no choice but to come to terms with the permanence of inequality in the only way acceptable to him, namely by means of the meritocratic argument. The meritocratic argument, incidentally, neatly takes care of another moral dilemma posed by our characters A and B. Suppose B, our underprivileged friend, was actually superior in intelligence to A? Doesn't this constitute a background advantage even more powerful than A's social-background advantage? If A is penalized for his superior social background, why isn't B penalized for his superior intellectual background? The answer here, of course, is that in the meritocratic utopia the only relevant quality in the treatment of individuals is their intelligence.

The dilemma of the liberal, backed into his meritocratic corner, would be the source of some concern had it not been for one simple fact: it is simply not true that education causes or explains mobility to any significant degree in industrial society. In spite of the high correlation between the distribution of material reward and the number of educational units achieved, there is really little causal link between the two. This is the great significance of Christopher Jencks's work.[8] Note that Jencks was not saying that education was unimportant: it certainly remains important in the society as the means of training people and enlarging the pool of technology. Nor was Jencks saying that education was not important for the mobile individual: it remains important as a certification of merit. Nor, further, was Jencks saying that education of itself was intrinsically insignificant: he made it clear that learning was intrinsically worthwhile and more of it could do no harm, and he also pointed out that since persons spent as much as a third of their lives in school it was obvious that the school environment ought to be taken seriously as an end in itself. What Jencks was denying—and I have read no persuasive refutation of the thesis—was the claim that there exists a causal relationship between education and the final reward, expressed in terms of income, of individuals. Beyond a certain point—a point which the vast majority of Americans pass—education as a factor in explaining the variance of income among individuals decreases rapidly to zero.

Jencks's work is as important for its negative findings as it is for its positive conclusions. One of these is the fact that we really don't know what accounts for the variance in income among individuals. Second, while we cannot explain income variance, we at least know some of the things that do not account for it. Education is one of these factors, as we have already indicated; another is family background. The latter is startling. One of the reasons why many have resisted this conclusion is the very biased nature of our perception of the inheritance of wealth. First, it is only the relatively few super-rich and their financial dynasties which stick in our minds when we think of the problem of inheritance. Second, as is true of human beings in every culture from the most primitive to the most advanced, there is a tendency toward what anthropologists call "telescoping" in our perception of corporate descent groups: that is, we keep track of those who remain in the group and simply neglect the many who drop out of it. In the case of rich families, these would be the downwardly mobile members of the family, and over time they would constitute the great majority of kinsmen.

If it is true that family characteristics play a minor role in the final distribution of income, this means that America has already achieved precisely what the liberals, backed into their defensive corner, have claimed as the last stronghold of justification for the educational institution as an agent of equalization. We don't need an agent for this purpose since it has already been achieved by means still to be determined.

To conclude, then, education not only has no effect on the structure of inequality in America and society in general (except for the most underdeveloped, "fourth-world" countries), it also has no effect on the direction and volume of mobility in such societies. And, what is more, in view of the fluidity of these systems, there is not much need remaining for any institution to play the role of facilitating mobility. To put it bluntly, with respect to equality education is either ineffective or irrelevant, or both.

In the light of these conclusions, it is clear that continuing to emphasize the role of education as a panacea for the inegalitarian ills of modern industrial society is simply an exercise in moral and sociological perversity. It may well be asked why it is that liberals have persisted with the doctrine. There are three reasons, I think: one is psychological, the second economic, and the third normative.

Psychologically, the reason for the persistence of the doctrine in the face of a mountain of findings contradicting it is to be found in the tendency of human beings to identify their own experience with the experience of the society in which they live. We like to see ourselves as a microcosm of the whole or, even better, we like to see our society as ourselves writ large. The reductionist fallacy springs from our deepest narcissistic impulses. Further, it is a fact that almost all those who reflect on, write about, or formulate policies on education are educators. What I am complaining about here is not just the fact that educators, being the only group in the community for whom the meritocracy argument has some substance, have projected their own experience on the rest of the society— this point we have made earlier. My present concern is the fact that educators have a vested interest in perpetuating the equal opportunity doctrine. American educators have been trapped by their own utilitarian justification for education. Instead of justifying expenditure on education on the ground that it is intrinsically good, an end in itself, as they should have done, educators and their liberal supporters have made all kinds of grand utilitarian claims for the institution, persuading politicians that it is the only sure weapon in the war on poverty, in exactly the same way the Pentagon lobbyists each year pressure the government into spending more money on some expensive new weapon on the grounds that it is the only surefire way to win a real war.

Because of the drastic demographic change in the U.S. population as the birth bulge of the forties passed through college, the politicians have already begun to cut back on school expenditures. For the politicians to learn now that education has little effect on the distribution of income in the society would, in the eyes of most educators, be a disaster. The professional educators, however, need have little worry, for the truth is that the entire American population has been sold on the idea that education is the path to equality. There is a nationwide confusion of a correlation with a causal relationship. And even when the confusion is suspected, it is not likely to be admitted, because no one likes to think that his or her success is due largely or even partly to luck or to such intangibles as being in the right place at the right time, having the right set of contacts, having a nice smile or a "nice guy" image. Instead, all Americans, and not just the educators, like to believe that they got where they are as a result of their intelligence, education, motivation, and hard work. The whole thing has become a rigidly established ideology, the latest secularization of the Calvinistic ethic. If we accept the fact that human beings need some system of rationalization to explain their lives and their destinies, that there is a strong human tendency to reject chance as a major force in the social universe, a tendency which even the great Einstein could not resist, we can understand how the liberal equal opportunity doctrine became so popular. It is America's secular faith, and as a tolerant man I could, under normal circumstances, simply wink at it and go about my business.

But alas, the circumstances are anything but normal, for when the equal opportunity doctrine goes beyond the middle classes and is wholly accepted by the poor and the dispossessed, especially that segment which is black, we are no longer dealing with a harmless bourgeois faith, but with the most sinister form of ideological mystification. It is striking that in the recent controversy surrounding Christopher Jencks's work the most vehement criticisms came from black scholars.[9] In addition to the reasons accounting for the persistence of the equal opportunity doctrine among whites, there are a few peculiar to blacks. One of these is that a critique of the doctrine robs blacks, especially black leadership, of both an easy and clear-cut definition of the root causes of their problems and the means of solving them. In the face of oppression the black leader cries, educate our children and we will be free. It never dawns on him that white children are being educated to the same extent as his own children and that, when the training is over, while his own and the white person's children will both be better off in absolute terms, their relative positions will have remained the same.

Another reason for black hostility to Jencks's radical critique of the equal opportunity doctrine is the fact that Jencks's work makes it painfully clear that while pockets of discrimination still exist, such discrimination applies to only a small minority of upper-middle-class blacks trying to break into the upper-middle echelons of the corporate structure. For the vast majority of the black

29

working and under class, discrimination is a non-problem. For many a young black school-leaver the problem does not even arise since there are no jobs around to apply for. The problem is not discrimination but the capitalist system and its merciless tendency toward the creation of structural unemployment. In this respect whites and blacks suffer alike.[10] It is one of the great ironies of South Boston that the Irish proles who are most violent in their defense of their cherished school system are those who are unemployed and who feel that the only chance for their children is a "good education," one which they think will be jeopardized by busing. No one has told them that it won't make a great deal of difference one way or the other, and if anyone did the chances are that he or she would be considered crazy.

So far, I have argued that there are psychological, ideological, and economic reasons why liberals and blacks, among others, hold to the equal opportunity doctrine. There is, however, another reason, one which is essentially ethical and which we have hinted at several times earlier but not explored. We are now thinking of the much-celebrated conflict between too much equality and the other liberal ideals, those involving the various freedoms.

The rights or freedoms that go to make up the libertarian ideal are of two basic types: one set involves freedom from certain kinds of constraints; the second set involves the rights to certain things.[11] Thus libertarians are strongly opposed to "big government," by which they mean a large, highly centralized governmental apparatus, their fear being that such governments tend to interfere too much with the free choice of individuals and tend to threaten both the right to private property and economic competition. The same fears account for the libertarian objection to big business, to overcentralization in the corporate structures, since this, it is claimed, leads to monopoly power and a restriction of economic freedom at both the production and consumption ends of the economy.[12]

Now what is interesting about all this is the way these negative freedoms relate to the positive freedoms of the libertarian. Among the most important of these are the freedoms to speak one's mind without fear of reprisals, to participate equally in the selection and influence of one's government, to enjoy one's property, and to receive equal and impartial treatment under the law. It should be noted immediately that all the positive freedoms are really egalitarian ideals expressed in libertarian language. We could describe all the positive freedoms as claims for equal distribution of certain rights. The point is that the set of positive freedoms is really just another expression of the egalitarian ideal, one, however, which carefully selects only those qualities for equal treatment which favor the rich and the powerful. We now know how the capitalist system solves the Aristotelian dilemma of determining criteria of relevance.

Even so, the obviously tendentious nature of the selection of the positive freedoms and the fact that it leaves the door open for an extension to other freedoms (at least theoretically) that may conflict with the interests of the establishment account for the fact that most conservative libertarians tend to emphasize only the negative freedoms. This, however, is a hopelessly weak and inconsistent position, because the truth is that the two sets of freedoms tend to be complementary. It is the positive freedoms that make the negative freedoms possible. If Ronald Reagan did not have the positive freedom of speech and political participation, he would not be able to run a campaign against centralized government and he would not be able to propagate policies aimed at increasing the degree of inequality and repression in the society.

Moreover, it should be pointed out that there is one freedom which stands above all others, but which libertarians are loathe ever to talk about, and this is the freedom to exercise one's particular freedoms. It cannot be denied that it is a cruel hoax to give a young Southern boy the right to use a swimming pool knowing that he will never be able to afford the entrance fee. Yet this is the position in which most of America's poor now find themselves. Clearly, the only way in which this most basic freedom can be achieved is through greater economic security.

True freedom, then, is not inconsistent with true equality. On the contrary, equality is a precondition for the effective exercise of one's freedoms. Taking away some, even if not all, of the power of the rich to deprive the poor of the effective exercise of their freedoms can hardly be called antilibertarian. And unless one perversely defines freedom as the right to deprive others of their freedom, there is no reason whatsoever why such egalitarianism should contradict any of the effective or theoretical rights of anyone.

Libertarians often assume that big governments and interference with positive personal freedoms go hand in hand. I have never read a persuasive defense of this assertion. It is true that a big government can become authoritarian, but one only has to examine a sample of the small nations of the United Nations with their equally small governments to realize that small governments are as prone to authoritarianism as big ones. It is not the size of a government which is critical in determining its libertarian or authoritarian tendencies, but its mode of selection and the degree of equality in the influence of its members on its policies.

While there is no causal relationship, indeed not even a correlation, between size and centralization of governments and their degree of authoritarianism, it is an established fact that the more centralized a government and the greater its control over the resources of a country, the greater the tendency toward equalization of wealth and, as a consequence, the greater the effective exercise of individual freedoms. Thus, in his comparative analysis of rich countries Harold L. Wilensky recently found that "the greater the authority of the central government vis-à-vis regional and local units, the higher the welfare state spending and the greater the program emphasis on equality."[13] It is no accident that the few libertarian gains made by blacks over the past few decades were achieved only after an epic struggle between the central government and the local authorities. Nor is it an accident that in the current presidential race the most reactionary elements—the antipoor, antiblack, and antiegalitarian—are those crying loudest for decentralization. Indeed the term decentralization and the anti-Washington sentiments now sweeping the country are simply the latest in a long line of code words which are to be translated as antipoor, antiblack, and antiegalitarian. They are not in the slightest degree concerned with freedom, for if the history of local and central governments in this country has taught us anything it is the fact that the most viciously authoritarian deprivation of human rights has always occurred at the state and municipal levels of government.

To conclude, then: the liberal fear that too great an effort in the direction of egalitarianism will conflict with other basic ideals and/or rights is a complete red herring. Equality is not inconsistent with freedom. Freedom is indeed partly a form of equality and partly a set of rights which require, for their effective enjoyment, greater equalization of wealth, status, and influence.

So far I have discussed the problem of equality mainly in terms made familiar by traditional theorists. The time has now come to shift our focus. We shall do this by posing a very blunt question, Why bother with equality if it is only or mainly the poor who are likely to benefit? Since the majority of persons living in most western industrial societies are doing all right for themselves, why shouldn't they simply turn their backs on the poor with the usual aside, "I'm all right, Jack"? If what has gone above is not to be a purely academic debate, it is important that we answer these questions.

The first thing to note about posing the problem in this way is that it introduces the concept of power, something lacking from the discussion so far. When we examine the role of power in western industrial societies what we find is a brutally simple moral formula: the control or ownership of property is might, and might is right. Because of the expansion of the middle classes in western industrial societies, the majority of persons have come to share the control and ownership of property, which determines might and right. Thus a kind of democracy thrives among the dictatorial majority. Even within this group it is recognized, however, that more property control and more might means more right. And between the dictatorial majority and the tyrannized minority of poor there is simply no question as to the absence of effective rights in one case and the monopolization of "right" in the other. This all comes out most clearly if we examine the workings of the institution which is supposed to be most sensitive to human rights, the courts. Numerous studies have now established the fact that the more wealth and power a person has the greater the tendency of the courts to view his action as right. Thus a lower-class man who steals $50 from a liquor store will be sent away for as much as ten years, while a white-collar criminal who steals a quarter of a million dollars from the assets of old widows is given a suspended sentence of six months.[14] If there was any residual doubt among the poor concerning the operation of the "might is right" principle, it was all dispelled with their observation of the Watergate trials and the treatments meted out to political criminals and ordinary criminals, whose crimes ranged from housebreaking to sedition.

The western industrial societies are, however, part of the community of civilized nations. A crude statement of the ethical truth of the system is ideologically intolerable. This is where the liberal intellectual and the school system with its equal opportunity doctrine become crucial. The liberal intelligentsia constitutes the conscience of western society. The liberal community becomes the superego of the body politic, constantly defining things as they should be, and, even more important, forever persuading itself and its captive audience—our schoolchildren—that what should be actually exists. It might not be perfect, but we are getting there. Michael Mann not long ago laid bare the real functions of the school system for the poor by showing how its emphasis on conservative, nationalistic values and uncritical approaches to learning produces graduates who have a wholly confused and unsystematic conception of their problems.[15] One finds an excellent example of this by examining the course curriculum of recent Afro-American studies programs. It is astonishing that the emphasis is overwhelmingly on the cultural, the historical, the traditional, and the mystical. There is very little concern with the hard-nosed problems of the economics of the black lower class. Indeed, the chairman of an Afro-American studies department at an Ivy League college which will remain nameless told a tutor in his department some years ago that blacks do not need to understand the economy to win their struggle for equality.

The drift of my argument so far has been in an extremely pessimistic direction. I could hardly help it. The problems of the poor, in spite of all sorts of talk and policy statements, are getting worse, not better. Inequality is presently on the increase in most western industrial societies, certainly in the United States. To make matters worse, a recent comparative study of affluent societies came up with the following depressing list of findings:

1. Correlates of affluence—a growing middle class, greater educational opportunity—will foster anti–welfare state ideologies.

2. The greater the educational opportunity, the more chance that the middle mass parents of college students as well as a large number of the highly educated will resist the push from below for equality.

3. The higher the rate of occupational mobility, the more chance that the mobile population will adhere to the success ideology.

4. The more social distance between the middle mass and the poor, the greater the resistance to spending that appears to favor the poor.[16]

If Wilensky is even half right the future of equality (and, thus, real freedom) looks none too bright in the western world. And yet I want to conclude that while the situation will no doubt be getting worse before it gets better (as the present reactionary wave that has swept not only the United States but even the Scandinavian welfare states works itself out) it will, eventually, improve. My reasons for thinking that the trend toward greater equality will eventually revive has nothing to do with the kind of arguments given by Clark Kerr and his associates.[17] I see no inherent structural tendency toward equality in western industrial society. What I see, in purely structural terms, is the emergence of an affluent majority, the hardening of its attitude toward the poor, and the imposition of a majorial tyranny in which the poor are increasingly ghettoized or cut off on reservations such as those of the Indians and the Appalachians.

The poor, however, have one last recourse, what I shall call their counter-leviathan power. Let me begin by specifying a few first principles. The primary instinct of human beings, as it is for all other animals, is self-preservation, and it is the social group that best insures the survival of the human animal. By what means, however, did human beings come together to insure their survival within groups? This is, of course, the old state-of-nature question, but it is one we can answer, if still only hypothetically, with more assurance today than when it was first posed. The famous Hobbesian answer is correct, but only partly correct. Human beings made an implicit contract to live together out of fear of the consequences of unrestrained freedom, and it is partly their fear of the leviathan power of the state which keeps them together in an ordered community.[18] There is, however, another basis of social life, and this is the almost instinctive assumption of equality. We see this from the most cursory observation of children. Interestingly, it would seem that it is not out of any instinctive sense of fairness that children share, but out of self-love and the avoidance of conflict, both of which, in turn, go back to the instinct for self-preservation. It is the urge to share, and, if possible, to share equally, that makes possible the other basis of group life—the thing that complements the leviathan—namely, consensus.

The basic problem of social science therefore is—or should be —to explain how inequality came into the world and how it is maintained. It is obviously well beyond the scope of this paper to undertake such a task. For our purposes, it is merely necessary to specify some of the major reasons why people accept unequal status and wealth. First, there is the fear of the leviathan, the organized force of the ruling class. Second, there is the sharing of nonmaterial values and beliefs—religion and the various secular creeds and ideologies. Third, individuals will accept inequalities if they perceive their society to be changing in such a way that there is an absolute increase in the standard of living. This is the main reason for the social stability of many societies undergoing rapid industrialization today, as it was of the Western European societies in the late eighteenth and nineteenth centuries.

Fourth, there is the technique of defining status in corporate rather than individual terms, with each group perceived as an essential and equal component of the body politic in spite of marked inequalities on the individual level. The classic example of this technique was the estate system of medieval Europe. We find, however, a revival of this method in the interest group politics of today. Thus workers and managers are treated as two equal corporate bodies at the highest levels of government and are so regarded by the press. It is clear, however, that this way of looking at equality benefits only the managers in the long run, because it means that the interests of a few people are equalized with the interests of millions and that the gross inequalities between individual members of one group and those of the other are completely neglected.

The final means of maintaining order involves an appeal to the sharing instinct. This is mobility and equal access reinforced by the equal opportunity doctrine. Up to a point, it would seem that individuals are prepared to accept inequality if they sincerely believe that they each have an equal shot at the success prize. The great advantage of this last technique, from a conservative standpoint, is that individuals have only themselves to blame for not making it.

As western societies became increasingly modernized, the accompanying trend toward secularization led to a decrease in reliance on the sharing of nonmaterial values. And as the growth rate peaked and levelled off, more and more persons began to consider their relative status as the crucial one in assessing their social condition. Corporate equality, while a convenient first step in the modern struggle of deprived groups, is soon recognized for the conservative strategy that it really is. The industrialization of the west, then, has meant that there has been a growing reliance on the leviathan power of the state and on mobility, with its accompanying equal opportunity doctrine, as the two basic means of maintaining order in the face of marked structural inequality. The more heterogeneous a society, and the less successful the realization of its equal opportunity ideal, the greater will be the reliance on force for the maintenance of order.

When the poor constituted a majority in modern society, there was always hope, if only in numbers. When, however, the poor are a minority, even a substantial one, they run the serious risk of being permanently neglected. They can only respond by utilizing their counter-leviathan power. The counter-leviathan power of the people is simply their capacity to undermine the system. It ranges, theoretically, on a continuum from exhortation and demonstration through to civil disobedience, riots, terrorism, and armed revolt. All this is fairly self-evident. What is more problematic is to pinpoint the range and type of resistance open to the poor, especially a minority poor. First, it is clear that the more violent extreme of the continuum is not perceived by the poor as either desirable or practicable. Outnumbered by a ratio of two to one and infinitely outgunned, the average poor man has too firm a grasp on reality to take revolutionary rhetoric seriously. True revolutions require, in addition to numbers, long-term planning and spartan discipline among the rebels and serious disunity among the ruling classes. None of these conditions apply to the United States or any of the Western European societies.

At the same time, and I am now thinking mainly of the United States, the more peaceful or primarily expressive forms of rebellion have already been used and are now exhausted as forms of protest. The civil rights movement in the United States is well and truly over. The black and Spanish-speaking middle classes have grown, and the poor now have rights in theory which they lack the means to enjoy.

This leaves the poor with a small middle range of counter-leviathan powers as the only means of protesting. What are these? They are primarily (1) criminal behavior, (2) cultural sabotage, and (3) economic sabotage. These three forms of counter-leviathan power have one thing in common: they are not conscious forms of collective behavior. There is no leadership, no ideology, no conscious effort to destroy the system. They are, instead, the additive action of millions of desperate, frustrated, and angry people. Often, their anger is turned everywhere except in the direction of their real object of frustration. It is turned against the self, against relatives and friends, and against the fellow poor. The affluent classes try to contain this potential destructiveness by pursuing policies leading to the ghettoization of the poor. Such policies largely succeed, but not entirely. And herein lies the problem for the affluent masses.

The poor cannot be entirely ghettoized. Invariably their crime spills over into the affluent suburbs. This is happening at an ever-increasing rate. Recent studies clearly indicate a shift in serious crimes from the inner cities to the suburbs. The passage of draconian laws fails to work because where there is not respect for the rule of law among the affluent, the poor can hardly be expected to take new laws seriously. Besides, laws are only as good as those who implement them, and as far as the poor are concerned the legal structure and law enforcement agencies of the United States are thoroughly corrupt.[19]

By cultural sabotage I mean the capacity of the poor to violate and debase the quality of life in a society. The poor are degraded and humiliated by their society and they, in turn, degrade it. All of us must at some time have driven through some slum or other and experienced a sense of terrible depression at the thought that fellow human beings are allowed, in the midst of affluence, to wallow in such abysmal squalor. Then there are the countless contacts we make with them on the streets, in the subways, at gas stations, contacts which always have an undertow of violence. Think of how we have come to take for granted the uncouth behavior of the big-city taxi driver. Or simply consider the general level of public intercourse. We fear the poor so much that we, the affluent, have come to fear ourselves. We do not know who to trust anymore. We hear a neighbor screaming and we close our windows.[20]

Again, there is the fact that the poor, where they exist in substantial numbers, as in America, come to influence greatly, and sometimes define, the lowest common denominator of popular culture and taste. The depressing state of American television is testimony to this fact. America has a much higher proportion of college-educated persons than any other society. And yet its programmers, in order to gain the attention of the culturally deprived lowest third, broadcast the most mindless drivel nightly. The same is true of consumer goods.

Economic sabotage comes about not through organized strikes but through the almost unwitting inefficiency of an unmotivated under class punctuated with intermittent wildcat strikes. Several European economies have come dangerously close to having the most sensitive sectors of their productive structures wholly dependent on immigrant labor. The dependency is not nearly so great in the United States, a substantial number of whose poor are unemployed. Even so, the role of unemployment as a source of poverty should not be exaggerated. It is a fact that the majority of poor in the United States are employed and their services are indispensable.[21] Without the poor worker the transportation, hospital, and sanitation systems, all essential for the survival of the major urban areas, would not be possible.

It is the capacity and willingness of the poor to debase and corrode the texture and style of industrial civilization which is the best argument for eliminating the group by making its members no longer poor. The alternative is a growing reliance on repressive policies which, while they will almost certainly fail, will be extremely expensive in terms of their costs in both money and personal freedom.

If and when the middle and upper classes come to see that it is in their own best interests to aim for a more egalitarian society, they will find a happy surprise waiting for them. When such a day comes it will be found that equality is the best guarantee for the preservation of all our basic freedoms, including the freedom to enjoy them all.

REFERENCES

1. Raymond Aron, *Progress & Disillusion: The Dialectics of Modern Society* (New York: Frederick A. Praeger, 1968), p. 1.

2. Since Michael Harrington's now-celebrated "discovery" of this problem there has been a vast outpouring of works on the subject. Of special value for our purposes are Joan Huber and Peter Chalfant, eds., *The Sociology of American Poverty* (Cambridge, Mass.: Schenkman, 1964); Harold L. Wilensky, *The Welfare State & Equality* (Berkeley: University of California Press, 1975); J. Larner and I. Howe, *Poverty: Views from the Left* (New York: William Morrow, 1965); and L. A. Ferman, J. L. Kornbluh et al., *Poverty in America* (Ann Arbor: University of Michigan Press, 1965).

3. Aristotle, *The Nicomachean Ethics,* Book V, esp. chaps. 6 and 7; Aristotle, *Politics,* Book III, esp. chap. 9. Two modern philosophical defenses of equality which we have found particularly helpful are J. Rawls, *A Theory of Justice* (Cambridge: Harvard University Press, 1971), esp. pp. 504-12; and H. Speigelberg, "A Defense of Human Equality," in W. T. Blackstone, ed., *The Concept of Equality* (Minneapolis: Burgess, 1969), pp. 144-64.

4. K. Davis and W. E. Moore, "Some Principles of Stratification," *American Sociological Review,* Apr., 1945.

5. Lee Rainwater, *Poverty, Living Standards & Family Well-Being,* Working Paper no. 10 (Cambridge, Mass.: Joint Center for Urban Studies, 1972).

6. For a critique of the "cult of education" among American students of developing countries, see Susanne J. Bodenheimer, *The Ideology of Developmentalism,* Sage Professional Papers in Comparative Politics, vol. 2, no. 01-105 (Beverly Hills, Calif.: Sage Publications, 1971), pp. 31-32.

7. See, for example, A. Stepan, "Political Development Theory: The Latin American Experience," *Journal of International Affairs,* 1966.

8. Christopher Jencks, *Inequality* (New York: Basic Books, 1972).

9. See *Perspectives on Inequality,* Reprint Series no. 8 (Cambridge: Harvard Educational Review, 1973).

10. See Stephan Thernstrom, "Is There Really a New Poor?," in Larner and Howe, *Poverty,* pp. 83-93.

11. I. Berlin, *Two Concepts of Liberty* (Oxford: Clarendon Press, 1958).

12. For different views on these issues, see *Commentary,* Sept., 1976.

13. Wilensky, *Welfare State & Equality,* p. 52.

14. R. Quinney, *The Social Reality of Crime* (Boston: Little, Brown, 1970).

15. Michael Mann, "The Social Cohesion of Liberal Democracy," *American Sociological Review,* vol. 35, no. 3 (June, 1970).

16. Wilensky, *Welfare State & Equality,* chap. 3.

17. C. Kerr, J. Dunlop et al., *Industrialism & Industrial Man* (New York: Oxford University Press, 1964).

18. Modern sociologists tend to avoid this subject. For a noteworthy exception, see William J. Goode, "The Place of Force in Human Society," *American Sociological Review,* vol. 37 (Oct., 1972), pp. 507-18.

19. See Edwin M. Schur, "Poverty, Violence and Crime in America," and Robert Vasoli, "Poverty and the Legal System," both in Huber and Chalfant, *Sociology of American Poverty.* See also Philip H. Ennis, "Criminal Victimization in the United States," in Lee Rainwater, ed., *Social Problems: Deviance and Liberty* (Chicago: Aldine, 1974), pp. 228-37; and Thomas Pettigrew, *A Profile of the Negro American* (Princeton, N.J.: D. Van Nostrand, 1964), pp. 136-56.

20. Even more significant is the fact that those charged with the "dirty work" of controlling the poor are increasingly revolting against their impossible position. See Everett C. Hughes, "Good People and Dirty Work," in Rainwater, *Social Problems: Deviance and Liberty,* pp. 335-42. See also Lee Rainwater, "Comment: The Revolt of the Dirty-Workers," *Transaction,* vol. 5 (Nov., 1967).

21. Barry Bluestone, "The Poor Who Have Jobs," in Huber and Chalfant, *Sociology of American Poverty,* pp. 140-53.

JAMES D. ANDERSON

Black Cultural Equality
in American Education

The Idea of Black Cultural Equality

The tenacious fight for black cultural equality by such serious and diverse scholars and leaders as W. E. B. Du Bois, Carter G. Woodson, Harold Cruse, Lerone Bennett, Stokely Carmichael, Malcolm X, and Vincent Harding (to name a few) should give us good reason to explore this theme in Afro-American thought. The black intelligentsia has been especially concerned with this question of human equality since the emancipation of the slaves. Indeed, many have viewed the struggle of blacks to gain equality of opportunity as one of the last great battles of American democracy. As we look back on the pursuit of equality in the black experience, however, we find that significant black leaders have defined equality of opportunity in terms very different from those of the majority society. The intellectuals and leaders of the dominant society have usually defined racial equality as the right of blacks to equal participation within the structure of Euro-American culture. They therefore view the removal of civil and political barriers as the end of discriminatory patterns in American society. In contrast to this view, Afro-American intellectuals and leaders have devoted considerable thought to the role of black culture in the existing or future socioeconomic arrangement. To be sure, Afro-Americans have been acutely aware of economic exploitation and political disfranchisement, and they have consistently proposed radical changes in the American political economy. Thus it would constitute a selective misreading of black history to argue that black

42

spokespersons have advocated cultural democracy to the exclusion or subordination of political and economic changes. In reality they have defined the fight for cultural equality in ways politically salient to the black struggle to attain material equality and also in a manner which prefigured the end of political and economic exploitation. In other words, black culture informs the struggle for political and economic equality and lays the foundation for institutional and social life in any new political economy.

The idea of black cultural equality is well illustrated in the thoughts of W. E. B. Du Bois. In an 1897 essay, "On the Conservation of the Races," he argued convincingly for the preservation and development of black culture.[1] Later he urged the young black writers of the 1920s to craft their politics from an examination of Afro-American culture and art.[2] Clearly, Du Bois never intended to subordinate the concrete reality of black economic exploitation to abstract and idealistic conceptions of Afro-American cultural uniqueness. In his monumental study of 1935, *Black Reconstruction,* he proposed the most sweeping and radical changes in the American and world economy. "A clear vision of a world without profit and of income based on work alone," wrote Du Bois, "is the path out, not only for America but for all men."[3] However, because of his understanding of the ideology and psychology of racism, Du Bois did not believe that a socialist economic system would necessarily eradicate the repression of black culture. Rather, he thought that the ideology of Euro-America (including its emerging radical segment), if strictly adhered to, would ultimately lead to the severe subordination or elimination of black culture in the interests of the white majority. For, as Du Bois viewed it, the variegated white leadership defined equality in a manner which assumed the immutability of Euro-American culture and which implied for blacks unilateral accommodation to the majority's conceptions of culture. Du Bois, however, maintained that Afro-American culture, embedded in the "marrow" of black bones, was an extraordinary view of the world and "the only path to a successful future."[4] Thus in his ninety-second year, before the 1960 Conference of the Association of [Black] Social Science Teachers, he reaffirmed his struggle to liberate black culture from the vortex of Euro-American repression. "What I have been fighting for and am still fighting for," said Du Bois, "is the possibility of black folk and their cultural patterns existing in America without discrimination; and on terms of equality."[5]

Du Bois was supported in his fight for black cultural equality by some of the most creative black intellectuals and leaders of the twentieth century. His contemporary Carter G. Woodson (1875-1950) was a dynamic spokesman and organizer for the preservation and development of black culture. He founded the Association for the Study of Afro-American Life and History (1915), the *Journal of Negro History* (1916), and the *Negro History Bulletin* (1937) to foster research and writings on black culture. Woodson was not as much an advocate of economic socialism as Du Bois, though he once stated that he had "no objection to this radical change" if it was carried out by intelligent and responsible leaders.[6] Woodson fully supported the idea of black cultural freedom and was one of the first to urge the inclusion of "Negro and African Philosophy and Art" in the black college and public school curriculums. Like Du Bois, he argued that "Negroes had their own ideas about the nature of the universe, time, and space, about appearance and reality, and about freedom and necessity."[7] Woodson saw in black culture the basis for an alternative world view that could challenge the dominance of the Euro-American outlook in the black community.[8]

Harold Cruse, former Marxist of the Old Left, in examining the complexity of black exploitation, concluded that "the greatest crime is that the Negro has been robbed of his cultural identity in America."[9] Cruse maintained that Afro-Americans could not hope to change society until they developed a comprehensive world outlook. To Cruse black liberation depended heavily on black cultural freedom, and he went so far as to argue that "without cultural equality there can be no economic and political equality."[10] Pan-Africanist Stokely Carmichael argued in the 1960s that the black struggle was primarily "a question of people fighting for their culture and their nature, fighting for their *humanity*."[11] Malcolm X echoed the same theme in the following way: "A race of people is like an individual man; until it uses its own talent, takes pride in its own history, expresses its own culture, affirms its own self-hood, it can never fulfill itself."[12] The theme of cultural equality has been repeated and elaborated in the writings of many contemporary black writers. It seems clear to such writers as Harold Cruse, Nathan Hare, and Vincent Harding that the questions of human equality and social arrangement cannot be understood apart from the question of culture. Moreover, to them any arrangement of American society is repressive as long as it fails to establish the equality of black culture.

Significantly, the proponents of black cultural equality have not viewed Afro-American culture as befitting the circumstances of blacks alone. They have maintained consistently that its real value lay in its potential contribution to a new humanity. Many students of Afro-American thought have missed this universal theme, however, and they have argued that the focus on black culture is too narrow, unsuited to advanced technological civilization, and hence a reactionary exercise in the glorification of race. But black intellectuals have thought invariably of the universal value of the Afro-American experience. To be sure, some black writers have been relatively quiet on this matter. They have had good reasons to be weary of universalism for, after all, black people have witnessed the misuse of such concepts in the hands of Western demagogues. Yet, as Du Bois stated in 1897, Afro-Americans believe "foolishly, perhaps, but fervently, that Negro blood has yet a message for the world."[13] "If black people duplicate the contributions of the world," said Carter G. Woodson, "the world will grow tired of such a monotonous performance." To Woodson, the world was "in need of vision and invention to give humanity something new." It was one of his fondest hopes that young black scholars and artists would penetrate their own experience and deliver to the world a profound message on bondage, freedom, and human equality. He prophesized in 1931 that "some Negro with unusual insight would write an epic of bondage and freedom which would take its place with those of Homer and Virgil. Some Negro with esthetic appreciation would construct from collected fragments of Negro music a grand opera that would move humanity to repentance. Some Negro of philosophic penetration would find a solace for the modern world in the soul of the Negro and then men would be men because they are men."[14] In a world of racism, exploitation, oppression, and domination, Du Bois and Woodson viewed the African drama in the New World as a great lesson for the human race. This universal concern undoubtedly solidified their commitment to preserve and develop black culture.

Nearly all of the writers who have demonstrated a commitment to black cultural equality have also shown great concern for the cultural basis of Afro-American education. The prospects for cultural freedom have been viewed as inseparable from an education grounded firmly on the accumulated wisdom derived from centuries of black life in America. Du Bois argued that "American Negroes have, because of their history, group experiences, and memories, a distinct entity, whose spirit and reaction demand a certain type of education for its development."[15] Carter G. Woodson was a sharp critic of the education which promoted Western "high culture" in black schools at the expense of the Afro-American tradition. He censored the black graduates of white colleges in the 1930s: "Negroes now studying dramatics go into our schools to reproduce Shakespeare, but mentally developed members of this race would see the possibilities of a greater drama in the tragedy of the man of color. Negroes graduating from conservatories of music dislike the singing of our folksongs. For some reason such misguided persons are insane enough to think that they can improve on the production of Shakespeare or render the music of foreign people better than they can themselves."[16]

The ideas of Woodson and Du Bois germinated slowly in the early twentieth century, but they have flowered in the contemporary black intellectual community. More recently, Lerone Bennett, in stating the "challenge of blackness," asserted that "we must conceive, conceptualize, and fight for a new rationality based on a new philosophy of education, conceived broadly as an instrument for social and personal change."[17] This new philosophy of education, according to Bennett, would relate learning to black culture and prescribe the institutionalization of the black experience in ways that could transform the thinking and acting of Afro-Americans. This is a widespread view among contemporary black educators, and it implies a complete restructuring of American education as it relates to Afro-American culture.[18]

The idea and implications of black cultural equality are very complex, but there are two specific concerns which appear most relevant to the contemporary debate over equality of opportunity and cultural pluralism. One challenge, put forth by Barbara A. Sizemore, contends that if culture provides the standards which are applied in evaluation processes, then blacks, with a distinctly different culture, can no longer allow Euro-America to "define their problems, create their values, and devise their norms."[19] This suggests that true equality of opportunity is the chance to be judged by the norms of one's own culture. This idea points toward giving authorities in Afro-American culture a position of parity and power to develop social and instructional norms for children within that cultural framework. This implies much more than the typical ethnic studies program which exists on the periphery of a school system based on the Euro-American culture. It calls for the transformation of Afro-American culture into instructional and social standards for evaluating the intellectual and social excellence of children (primarily black children) within the context of that culture. Unfortunately, there have been few attempts to accomplish this, though it has been consistently alluded to in the literary and intellectual writings of Afro-Americans.

A second concern deals with the distribution of resources and academic authority in American education. If the principle of difference in national culture and tradition is recognized, it then becomes a basis for reforming educational resource allocation and academic authority. The reality of diverse cultures suggests a system of multiple norms, which, in turn, implies an academic community of multiple credentialing groups. At the very least, the new system would need an academic community that is cross-culturally competent. In any case, the "authority of the learned" in Afro-American culture would require the power to evaluate and credential students according to their performance within the structure of Afro-American culture. Similarly, the case for allocating educational resources would rest significantly on the logic that schools preserve and develop cultures and, therefore, that public money ought to be equitably distributed for the support of varied national cultures. At first glance, this may appear as a demand for equality of results. Yet it merely calls for equality of opportunity, the equal chance to perform and be judged by the standards of one's own culture, in other words, the type of opportunity that Euro-Americans have enjoyed since the founding of the nation. The equality of condition for all individuals has sometimes been opposed on the grounds that some individuals are more meritorious than others, and should thus have the right to become unequal. It seems to follow, then, that if cultures are of equal merit, one is perfectly justified in asking that public resources be equitably distributed for their maintenance and development. In short, cultural egalitarianism appears to affirm rather than undermine the idea of equality of opportunity for individuals. A more or less equal chance in the educational system, made possible by relating cultural norms to school norms, would enhance equality of opportunity for individuals.

Black scholars have also recognized the intellectual challenge inherent in the idea of black cultural freedom and equality. Lerone Bennett presents this challenge in its clearest form while juxtaposing Afro-American reality with the "American Ideal":

> We cannot deal with black experience until we realize that the black experience raises fundamental questions about the total historic process, and that it requires a radical re-evaluation of our ideas about history and man. In its essence, the black experience is a radical re-appraisal of a society from the standpoint of the men on the bottom. . . . Because of who they [blacks] are and what they have been through, because of the irrefutable evidence of their scars, they are the creative negation of all the placid myths about American society. . . . Blackness is a challenge, then, to America and to all its institutions and values.[20]

Bennett and many other black writers believe that the black experience should raise fundamental questions about the meaning of American education. Essentially, this is a call for black intellectuals to challenge the very meaning of American life and culture as traditionally defined by the established intellectual community. This concern goes far beyond the school's role in teaching children to read and calculate to a consideration of the institution as the only organized means of shaping the world view and character of the young. Such concerns bring us to a number of difficult problems which the idea of black cultural equality poses for the existing educational system.

Black Culture and the Educational Process

The current concerns about the social organization of the public schools have been generated largely by the political and intellectual challenges of Native Americans, Spanish-speaking Americans, and Afro-Americans. To be sure, it is true that European ethnic groups now represent themselves as distinct cultural groups,[21] but it is unthinkable that we would now witness sustained movements to change the social setting of education were it not for the minority political and intellectual movements of the last decade. In the 1960s the social organization of the school assumed an enormous new importance for blacks, Puerto Ricans, Mexican-Americans, and Indians. The roots of the crisis were old, and the realization that schools could not effect mass economic mobility facilitated an increased emphasis on schools as the organized means of inducting the young into the culture. Such a realization posed anew the important question, what culture?

The new focus on American education revealed that the schools, on balance, were products of Euro-American culture and reflected the dominant group's criteria for judgment of value and performance. The selected elements of Euro-American culture, history, and common social characteristics and the psychological dimension of identity, rituals, and ceremonies constitute the basis of the educational process. Therefore, the cultural process of schooling gained importance as studies showed that learning was significantly related to the culture structure of the school setting.[22] It was demonstrated that the norms for school activities and rewards and the standards for instruction are heavily influenced by sociocultural origins. Moreover, the cultural content selected for instructional purposes essentially indicated the things deemed worthwhile by the dominant ethnic group. The standards for competence, efficiency, and hard work in school as well as the general goals of education reflected the common history, traditions, and aspirations of Euro-America.

Even the teachers and staff from different backgrounds tended to represent the dominant culture. From the vantage point of many minorities, then, the American school setting mirrored primarily the parochialism (or universalism) of the dominant culture.

Previous concerns for the cultural organization of schools had been set aside as educators stressed the importance of improving the ability of minority children to read and calculate. Compensatory educational programs were deemed more important than programs aimed at fundamental cultural change. The failure of compensatory educational programs to alter the performance of minority children and the realization that schools could not deliver on promises of better jobs and college admission opened the way for humanistic considerations of educational policy. Attention then turned to the fact that schools deal more with the shaping of character, social role selection, and political socialization than with material advancement. The shift in educational instruction from concrete facts to aesthetic judgment, interpretation, and philosophical analysis increased the concern for the cultural basis of the educational process. With mathematics there was no problem, but language, history, literature, art, dance, music, civics, politics, etc., provoked great concern. The nature of the school's social norms drew more attention than the instructional norms. There emerged minority movements to control schools largely affecting their children and demands for ethnically oriented curricula if not entire school systems. These demands have brought blacks, Indians, Puerto Ricans, and Mexican-Americans into conflict with the dominant educational establishment.

This conflict revolves, in part, around political-ideological differences and conflicting perceptions of the real nature of the school setting. Those in control of the educational system assert that schools are open to all and that students are limited mainly by their motivation and mental capacity. In spite of the parochial reality of the Euro-American–based educational system, educators tend to recognize schooling as a force of secularism, rationality, and, above all, universalism. The schooling process is approached as a means of transformation from the family and community to the order of the nation, where ethnic and folk cultures have no significant influence.

Many educators assume that schools release individuals from the statuses and identities forged by ethnic origin and assign new roles according to how well they learn to read and calculate. The ideology, at least, is one of equal opportunity, pretending that everyone's advancement depends largely on personal rather than cultural qualities. The experiences of Chinese, Japanese, and Jews—who have done well in schools in the absence of any public recognition of their culture—are presented as evidence that schools are committed to honest teaching and offer no significant advantages to the adherents of particular cultures. In short, with regard to the question of whether cultural recognition is important to success in schools, educators generally hold that it is not. It must be noted, however, that academic performance may not shed any light on cultural well-being. Moreover, the experiences of smaller groups like the Japanese, Armenians, Greeks, and Jews have been profoundly different from those of larger ethnic groups and national minorities. The larger Eastern European groups have not been noted for rapid progress in schools, and America's national minorities, Spanish-speaking Americans, Afro-Americans, and Native Americans—who have been here from the colonial beginnings—have experienced an even more separate and distinct development. Yet educators hold that these groups should follow the path of the Japanese, Armenians, and Jews. This approach is evidence of their belief that group character and cultural background should not be interwoven into the educational system, except in the case of the dominant culture and ethnic group.[23]

From the vantage point of Afro-Americans, the school setting is inequitably and inhumanely ethnocentric. The public school systems repress the black heritage as though it were dysfunctional and destined to disappear. Where education is concerned, therefore, Afro-Americans feel that they are more truly deprived than the adherents of the dominant culture.[24] A pragmatic argument for changing the school setting is based on the claim that the social norms of schooling alienate black children.[25] This alienation presents problems beyond the question of academic success. Minority students who are successful at achieving the instructional norms of the school still complain of the cultural sacrifices they were compelled to make in order to meet the social and cultural standards of those in power. Richard Rodriguez contends that the school confronted him with the choice of being an "intellectual" or a Chicano. He accepted the socialization of the school and "had to forget most of what my culture had provided, because to remember it was a disadvantage."[26] The consciousness of minority children, like that of the majority, is not merely individual: it embodies the culture of the society in which the child participates and the social relations which are formed within the family, community, and racial or ethnic group. Afro-American pupils, despite their academic performance, are alienated by school environments which force them to deny or denigrate their cultural backgrounds.[27]

Under the mythology of cultural neutrality, the school system practices cultural hegemony and makes socialization into the dominant culture a prerequisite for occupational achievement and upward social mobility. It uses the largely false promises of better jobs and college admission as levers to coerce black students to accept Euro-American acculturation as necessary for social advancement. School administrators help to identify and promote the goals of the dominant culture, and they also determine and operationalize the means for modifying and shaping that culture. These actions have little to do with concerns for the ability to read and calculate. The main concern is with the way of life that Euro-America wishes to foster for its own benefit and as a basis for a national culture. The cultural development of Afro-America is viewed as antagonistic to Euro-American hegemony and, therefore, to national unity. The "Americanization" program for immigrants deliberately destroyed languages and cultures in the name of securing allegiance to the United States. Now educators and social scientists fear that Native Americans, Spanish-speaking Americans, and Afro-Americans will undo this unity. Nathan Glazer fears that in an ethnically oriented school system "we risk losing the sense of the United States as a country dedicated from its birth to distinctive and great ideals."[28] One quickly realizes that the concern here is for national unity and emotional attachment to the "American Ideal." Indeed, one would have to suppress or greatly distort the past of Native Americans, for example, to convince them that

America was "dedicated from its birth to distinctive and great ideals." Similarly, Afro-Americans have much to say about the distinctiveness of slavery and the "great" ideals that supported it. It is easy to see how eagerness for national unity and fear of alternative views of the world have driven educators and social scientists to oppose the inclusion of minority culture into the core of the educational process. As sociologist Orlando Patterson contends, "No nation can be sustained by a culture that is simply a grotesque potpourri of the patterns of every imaginable tribal group, all jostling with one another for a place on the national table for their own cherished recipe."[29] Patterson has clearly exaggerated minority demands, but he has aptly stated his fear that "pluralism works actively against the emergence of that moral constitution that American society now so badly needs to support the high ideals of its legal constitution."[30] Patterson therefore maintains that "the only alternative is a return to the idea of cosmopolitanism."

The positions of Patterson and Glazer on the place of minority culture in the school setting are explicitly linked to their political-ideological concerns for a culture to sustain the nation and to their commitment to promote common political values. It is largely on these grounds that they justify restricting minority cultures to an insignificant role in the educational mainstream. Glazer urges a reconsideration of "afternoon schools" and "parochial schools" as mechanisms for reconciling the demands and needs of minority communities with those of the larger community.[31] He views this as a means of preventing the problems of minority cultural development from being imported into the work of the public school. Patterson calls for a complete rejection of minority cultures. He prescribes a universalist norm whereby the performances of all children are judged by a single standard of efficiency and competence and forms of social conditioning congruent with the work ethic.[32] This appeal to universalism either ignores or unquestioningly accepts the Euro-American orientation of the existing school system. Certainly Patterson must know that conceptions of work, efficiency, and competence are relative to cultural origins. His effort to promote Euro-American values to the level of universalism is mainly an attempt to legitimize the dominant culture as the only national culture. Such rationalization fits well with his political-ideological goals. It also attempts to justify the use of political and economic institutions, the mass media, and the schools to ceaselessly force conformity and standardization on those who do not adhere to the same political or cultural goals. Patterson's political-ideological goals are at variance with the interests of Afro-Americans and other minorities who feel their needs and cultures should significantly shape the structure of America's social institutions.

Afro-Americans (as well as Native Americans and Spanish-speaking Americans) are now engaged in a struggle to redefine the function of educational institutions and the schools' responsibilities to separate national cultures. These concerns have gone far beyond the question of material advancement to a consideration of the educational meaning of diverse national cultures. Blacks are now demanding for their children an educational setting grounded firmly in the distinctiveness of their native cultural background. This demand is probably motivated by something much deeper than concerns for school achievement and self-identity. Afro-Americans are convinced of the intellectual and humanizing potency of their own experiences. They view their own culture as having great integrity and contend that it offers insights as intellectually profound and as "universal" as those of the dominant culture. Thus blacks wish to transform their cultures from the folk level into visible forms of social and institutional life. In this context the Afro-American challenge to American education is much more than a quest for social mobility. The values at stake are not so much material and economic as they are cultural, ethical, and aesthetic. The aim is not to mimic the education that exists but to turn over a new leaf, work out new concepts, and try to set afoot a new education based on the common experiences and aspirations of black people.[33] Some of these goals may meld with the objectives of traditional institutions. The attempt to socialize black children into the dominant life styles, however, is at variance with the interests of important segments of the Afro-American community. The educational establishment views the schools as ineffective because they fail to implant the values of the dominant culture into the minds of black children; many black intellectuals, on the other hand, feel that the schools are badly organized and inefficient but, more important, that they lack legitimacy because of their role in cultural oppression. As one writer put it, the schools contribute "to the progessive alienation of Afro-American school children."[34] The existing standards of public education are being rejected in search of standards more reflective of the diverse cultures in the nation. The changes sought are cultural, then, rather than tactical. Hence even better performance under the existing standards may not satisfy black demands for a fundamental restructuring of the school setting.

The real questions for schooling have not yet been raised, and the deepest problems have not yet been faced. The present commitment to black culture is at best half-hearted, and school officials rush to define acceptable aspects of the culture so as to incorporate the "quaint" rather than the "threatening." The most liberal architects of cultural innovation seem to base their prescriptions on concerns for social prestige, economic mobility, and a common national culture. The basic concern is for a school setting that prepares minority children for "acceptance" in the mainstream. Cultural pluralist Michael Novak argues that "power in America is essentially Anglo-American, hence it is a condition of survival (and eventual justice) that all the others penetrate the intricacies of the Anglo-American mind."[35] School officials use a similar rationale for imposing the dominant culture on black school children. On the question of language, Odis Rhodes argues that "if black youngsters are to have any hope of upward mobility, they must learn to speak a socially acceptable dialect—the standard English dialect."[36] Learning standard English may be a desirable goal, but Rhodes's justification is severely flawed and misleading as a basis for educational prescriptions. If black children were to study those things which are "socially acceptable," they would study very little about themselves, because Afro-American culture is still downgraded by those who control the rewards in schools and society. Similarly, if blacks followed Novak's advice to "penetrate the intricacies of the Anglo-American mind," little time would be left to penetrate the depths of their own culture. Moreover, neither of the recommendations will elevate considerable numbers into higher status levels in the society, so the argument of mass economic mobility is really a false one.[37] The linking of education to the myth of mass social mobility, however, compels both pluralists and universalists to accept the idea of achieving uniform results. The universalists advocate mainstream culture on the basis of its inexhaustible wisdom, insight, and national standards, while the pluralists advocate the same on the grounds of upward mobility and social approval. The latter, however, pay tribute to quaint aspects of minority culture en route to the mainstream. This commitment to the mainstream in education leads inevitably to a perpetuation of the prevailing school structure. If the mainstream is essentially Anglo-American, it follows that the quickest path to the mainstream is through a system based primarily on Anglo-American social norms.

It is necessary, then, when considering the social organization of the school, to pay considerable attention to the cultural purposes of education in black communities. Institutional policies set structure, define roles, and allocate resources for development. A school system aimed at promoting black culture implies a different social setting than one designed to relegate that culture to a secondary or ceremonial status. A school system which attempts to mold a basic value consensus will operate differently from one that seeks to house and foster diverse value orientations. The notions that organic communities of interest hold legitimate claims on the school setting and that school norms should derive significantly from different cultures call for a new arrangement of the school system. In short, educational policy aimed at promoting black culture would differ sharply from policy intended to arrest the development of black cultural patterns.

Harold Cruse has written extensively about the deliberate degradation and suppression of black culture.[38] Likewise, Frank Kofsky traced the exploitation and humiliation of black culture in the world of jazz. Kofsky found few attempts to encourage black art and culture. The general practice of whites, who controlled the economic resources, was to concentrate on the commercial profits derived from black talent. Those outside of the jazz milieu generally felt that black art was beneath serious consideration. As Kofsky wrote: "Even now, in 1969, for all of the supposedly greater acceptance of black art and culture this country is said to have achieved, only a single black musician, Ornette Coleman, has ever been the recipient of a Guggenheim Foundation award for his work in jazz."[39] The school system, unfortunately, reflects the sentiment of the dominant society. It has been resistant to the development of Afro-American culture—making only those innovations necessary to quell black protest without fundamentally affecting the traditional character of the school setting. These small changes appear pluralist while perpetuating, through new complexities, "the old assimilationist program."

Any move toward a public policy which supports the development of diverse cultures depends, in part, on the destruction of the myth that schools effect mass social mobility. This myth has been the major rationale for enforcing conformity and standardization on Afro-American children. It is argued that the economic mainstream is Euro-American and, therefore, blacks will get better jobs when they receive adequate educational preparation in the norms of Euro-American cultures, but recent studies are demonstrating that schools cannot effect mass economic mobility. Educators and social scientists still persist, however, in their efforts to penetrate the depths of Afro-American behavior in order to create programs that will "utilize the child's differences as a means of furthering his acculturation to the mainstream while maintaining his individual identity and cultural heritage."[40] The major emphasis is on acculturation and hence the danger exists that Afro-American culture will be examined to develop communication lines to more easily co-opt black pupils into mainstream values. In this drive the "pluralist" model would be applied to the serious detriment of black cultural development. Anthropologists Charles and Betty Lou Valentine already fear that "respect for sub-cultural systems as legitimate human creations, which is communicated with the difference model, will be accorded no more than lip service."[41] The proponents of the pluralist model, having misperceived the fundamental causes of Afro-American social conditions, tend to think that social mobility for blacks turns on the question of competence in mainstream cultural styles. It turns instead on racial and class barriers that inhibit the opportunity to practice alternative cultural patterns actively.[42] Teachers and educational specialists concentrate on giving blacks new skills and cultural styles while ignoring the fact that they suffer mainly from political and economic repression in spite of cultural competencies. A real cultural awareness program might focus on the institutional racism which limits the opportunity of Afro-Americans to practice the skills and cultural styles that they already possess.

The Challenge to Black Intellectuals

The resolution of the educational and cultural problems posed by Afro-Americans and other national minorities will not be an easy task. Afro-Americans, and Native Americans, are not merely ethnically distinct; they constitute a separate national culture that has remained fundamentally apart from the Euro-American experience. To be sure, they have contributed to the development of American nationality as a whole, but while absorbing some basic elements of Euro-American culture they have developed a separate culture of their own. Though many intellectuals of the dominant ethnic group continue to argue that Afro-Americans do not constitute a distinctive national culture, the onslaught of recent scholarship is rapidly exposing the weakness of this position.[43] Until about ten years ago, Afro-American history and culture held little or no interest for white scholars. Now a considerable number of them are attempting to understand black religion, music, folklore, dance, language, drama, literature, and family life from an Afro-American perspective and world view. Afro-American scholars, however, have long explored the cultural dimension of their history. It is time for black scholars to take the next step and make clear what sort of standards should serve as social and instructional norms for value judgments within Afro-American cultural structures. The task calls for a complete restructuring of the instructional and cultural norms of the school system.

Black intellectuals who are committed to the idea of Afro-American cultural freedom and equality must also work toward the refinement of a democratic social philosophy which will prescribe the removal of color discrimination and affirm the right of equal cultural representation. To do this is not easy. The dominant Euro-American intelligentsia will argue that such a conception of social arrangement clashes with the "American Ideal" of achievement and equality which allegedly denies the importance of ethnic and racial differences in public policy. Nathan Glazer, in a recent book on ethnic inequality and public policy, has argued that state policy organized around group distinctiveness is anti-American. The American ethnic ideal, he asserts, is a policy of "salutary neglect"; "any ethnic group could maintain itself, if it so wished, on a *voluntary* basis."[44] To Glazer, the nation was meant to be "a republic of states" and "the states were not to be carriers of an ethnic or national pattern." Black intellectuals must make it clear that this is a view of America which assumes, consciously or unconsciously, that all Americans are "ethnic" except Anglo-Americans. Clearly, the states have given full support to the preservation and development of Anglo-American culture and that culture did not come to engulf the institutions of this nation on a voluntary basis. For example, consider the case of the public state universities. It makes no sense to argue that the Euro-American departments of dance, folklore, literature, music, languages, religion, history, art, etc., were established on a voluntary basis. Rather, their establishment was a classic case of Euro-American leaders and intellectuals making claims on public money for the preservation and development of their own culture. It made no difference to them that much of the capital used for this development was accumulated on the backs of African slaves. In time, they came to view the over-representation of Euro-American culture as the natural and irreversible order of society and apparently forgot that it achieved its dominance through the use of state power and public money. But Du Bois and Woodson, unlike Glazer, did not forget how this dominance was achieved, and they felt quite legitimate and American in making claims on public money for equal cultural representation. Following the tradition of such black scholars, contemporary black intellectuals should continue to point out that public support for the development of Afro-American culture is no less legitimate than the public money traditionally given for the maintenance of Euro-American culture.

We should also be concerned with those (especially black scholars) who will reject the idea of black cultural equality in favor of

EQUALITY AND SOCIAL POLICY

the "cosmopolitan" idea. It is not clear that this implies anything more than a reaffirmation of Western "high culture," but it is quite apparent that there has been no cosmopolitan idea in America which included the cultures of Indians, blacks, Puerto Ricans, or Mexican-Americans. Moreover, it is equally apparent that cosmopolitanism is not the language of oppressed groups and that it usually issues from those in positions of power. The American rhetoric of cosmopolitanism increased as the nation became a world power. Its leaders now discuss universalism and world order from positions of national freedom and equality. Cosmopolitanism is primarily the velvet glove of diplomacy over the fist of state power, and when its advocates are threatened they resort not to rationality but to war. Black intellectuals need not reject cosmopolitanism; they must simply put the idea in its proper perspective. If they want to extend cosmopolitanism they must first establish the cultural freedom and equality of their own oppressed group. Then they can join the cosmopolitan group.

Black intellectuals will also have to contend with the economic determinists, who argue that black cultural freedom will come into existence with a radically new economic system. This view, however, fails to grapple with the persuasive scholarship that demonstrates the autonomous nature of racist ideology. Scholars like David Brion Davis, Winthrop D. Jordan, and Charles Lyons have shown that anti-black prejudice existed in Europe and New England prior to the existence of slavery.[45] There is no guarantee that racism, and hence the repression of black culture, will not continue under a new socioeconomic arrangement. The prospects for black cultural freedom depend significantly on the effective elimination of the racist element in Euro-American thought.

Perhaps the most dogged resistance to black cultural equality will come from a class of neoconservative intellectuals who were strangely traumatized by the black political, literary, and intellectual movements of the mid-sixties.[46] Couching their resistance in concerns for meritocracy and public order, these intellectuals argue that any public recognition and support of Afro-American culture will cause many groups (especially "white ethnics") to emerge with the same demands. According to Nathan Glazer, since "the Negroes became blacks" and demanded their "proper share of power and wealth," the blue-collar and lower-middle-class whites have begun to rehabilitate their own ethnic identities as a means of protecting and extending their positions. Glazer maintains that "from the mid-sixties . . . the ethnic identity began to gain on the general American identity." Glazer and other neoconservatives perceive that the Afro-American emphasis on cultural distinctiveness has legitimated the rise of widespread ethnic identity which is pushing America toward being a nation of conflicting "tribal" groups. Glazer's own conclusion, however, is that the white ethnic reaction is not connected to any sincere desire for distinct cultural representation. To Glazer, the white ethnics have no "strong concerns for the maintenance of the specifically cultural aspect of the ethnic heritage." The white ethnics are demanding symbolic recognition of their heritage; there are no "distinctive white ethnic cultures among the later groups [immigration after 1880 or 1890] that they particularly wish to defend." The white ethnic movement was primarily a defensive reflex that was generated by the understanding or misunderstanding that blacks were gaining at the expense of whites. The response was largely one of political opportunism, frequently informed by racial prejudice, and held no important ramifications for the cultural restructuring of social and institutional life in America. It makes no sense, therefore, that neoconservative intellectuals should be terribly concerned about having to recognize distinctive white ethnic cultures when, according to their own arguments, they do not believe that such cultures exist in any significant forms.[47]

Nevertheless, these neoconservative intellectuals are using the white reaction as a rationale to argue against the public recognition and support of Afro-American culture. This is primarily an alarmist argument, and the suggestion that group demands will destroy public order overlooks the long-established right of "compelling state interest" to override group liberty when the state's legitimate interest is really threatened. However, in the opinion of the United States Supreme Court, "only the gravest abuses, endangering paramount interests, give occasion for permissible limitation."[48] Thus if a person sacrifices human beings in his backyard as a part of his religion, he is confronting the interest of the state in protecting human life; in such a case the state may limit the person's exercise of religion. The demand for Afro-American cultural equality is not, however, a threat to public order; instead, it is a threat to the hegemony of the Euro-American intelligentsia in controlling and defining the nature of American life and culture. But rather than fighting the battle on its legitimate terrain, these intellectuals have falsely charged that black intellectuals are undermining the "American Ideal."

The Afro-American intelligentsia should support the laws which forbid the exclusion of blacks from public programs, and with equal force they should challenge the laws or customs which compel the inclusion of blacks into a system whose inevitable effect is to shape the opinions and values of their children into the standard Euro-American mold. Traditionally the nation has resolved this problem by admitting diversity for those who could afford private education, but the fact that cultural diversity, largely a euphemism for non–Euro-American, is relegated to private society simply underscores the reality that Euro-American values are advanced by state power and public money. The state nowhere explicitly claims that it has a right to obliterate cultural differences, or to acculturate minority children into Euro-American life styles, yet the dominant intelligentsia has historically used the schools for this purpose. It is here, therefore, in the realm of state power and wealth, that the Afro-American intelligentsia should insist upon a public policy of equal cultural representation.[49]

REFERENCES

1. W. E. B. Du Bois, "On the Conservation of the Races," in John A. Bracey, August Meier, and Elliot Rudwick, eds., *Black Nationalism in America* (New York: Bobbs-Merrill, 1970), p. 256.

2. W. E. B. Du Bois, "Criteria for Negro Art," in Meyer Weinberg, ed., *W. E. B. Du Bois: A Reader* (New York: Harper and Row, 1970), p. 251.

3. W. E. B. Du Bois, *Black Reconstruction in America, 1860-1880* (New York: Harcourt, Brace, 1935; repr. ed., Cleveland: Meridian Books, 1964), pp. 706-7.

4. W. E. B. Du Bois, "The Future and Function of the Private Negro College," in W. E. B. Du Bois, *The Education of Black People: Ten Critiques, 1906-1960,* ed. Herbert Aptheker (Amherst: University of Massachusetts Press, 1973), pp. 143-44.

5. Du Bois, "Future and Function of the Private Negro College," p. 150.

6. *New York Age* (Jan. 21, 1932).

7. *New York Age* (Nov. 1, 1932); see also Carter G. Woodson, *The Mis-Education of the Negro* (Washington, D.C.: Associated Publishers, 1933).

8. Lerone Bennett, *The Challenge of Blackness* (Atlanta: Institute of the Black World, 1970), p. 11.

9. Harold Cruse, *Rebellion or Revolution* (New York: William Morrow, 1968), pp. 245-46.

10. Cruse, *Rebellion or Revolution,* p. 247.

11. Stokely Carmichael, *Stokely Speaks* (New York: Vintage Books, 1971), p. 121.

12. George Breitman, *The Last Year of Malcolm X* (New York: Schocken Books, 1968), pp. 110-11.

13. W. E. B. Du Bois, "Strivings of the Negro People," *Atlanta Monthly,* vol. 80 (Aug., 1897), p. 195.

14. *New York Age* (May 23, 1931).

15. W. E. B. Du Bois, "Does the Negro Need Separate Schools?," *Journal of Negro Education,* vol. 4 (July, 1935), p. 330.

16. *New York Age* (May 23, 1931); Michael R. Winston, "Carter Godwin Woodson: Prophet of a Black Tradition," *Journal of Negro History,* vol. 60 (Oct., 1975), pp. 462-63.

17. Bennett, *Challenge of Blackness,* p. 5.

18. Nathan Wright, ed., *What Black Educators Are Saying* (New York: Hawthorn Books, 1970); "The Future of Education for Black Americans," special issue of *School Review,* vol. 81 (May, 1973); Jim Haskins, ed., *Black Manifesto for Education* (New York: William Morrow, 1973); *Education and Black Struggle: Notes from the Colonized World,* Harvard Educational Review Monograph No. 2 (Cambridge: Institute of the Black World, 1974); Edgar G. Epps, ed., *Cultural Pluralism* (Berkeley: McCutchan, 1974), see pt. 2, "Black Experience: Segregation to Community Control."

19. Barbara A. Sizemore, "Making the Schools a Vehicle for Cultural Pluralism," in Epps, *Cultural Pluralism.*

20. Bennett, *Challenge of Blackness,* p. 8; Vincent Harding, "The Vocation of the Black Scholar and the Struggles of the Black Community," in *Education and Black Struggle,* pp. 1-29.

21. Nathan Glazer, "Ethnicity and the Schools," *Commentary,* vol. 58 (Sept., 1974), pp. 55-59; Nathan Glazer and Daniel P. Moynihan, eds., *Ethnicity: Theory and Experience* (Cambridge: Harvard University Press, 1975).

22. Robert Dreeban, *On What Is Learned in School* (Reading, Mass.: Addison Wesley, 1968); Patricia Cayo Sexton, *The American School: A Sociological Analysis* (Englewood Cliffs, N.J.: Prentice-Hall, 1967).

23. Leonard J. Fein, "Community Schools and Social Theory: The Limits of Universalism," in Henry M. Levin, ed., *Community Control of Schools* (New York: Simon and Schuster, 1970).

24. Glazer, "Ethnicity and the Schools."

25. Charles A. Valentine, "Deficit, Difference, and Bicultural Models of Afro-American Behavior," *Harvard Educational Review,* vol. 41, no. 2 (May, 1971), pp. 137-57; Diana T. Slaughter, "Alienation of Afro-American Chil-

dren: Curriculum and Evaluation in American Schools," in Epps, *Cultural Pluralism.*

26. Richard Rodriguez, "On Becoming a Chicano," *Saturday Review* (Feb. 28, 1975), p. 46; Michael Novak, "One Species, Many Cultures," *American Scholar,* vol. 43, no. 1 (Winter, 1973-74); Normal J. Johnson, "About This Thing Called Ghetto Education," in John F. Szwed, ed., *Black America* (New York: Basic Books, 1970).

27. Slaughter, "Alienation of Afro-American Children," p. 144.

28. Glazer, "Ethnicity and the Schools," p. 59.

29. Orlando Patterson, "On Guilt, Relativism, and Black-White Relations," *American Scholar,* vol. 43, no. 1 (Winter, 1973-74), p. 128.

30. Patterson, "On Guilt, Relativism, and Black-White Relations," p. 130.

31. Glazer, "Ethnicity and the Schools," p. 59.

32. Patterson, "On Guilt, Relativism, and Black-White Relations," p. 131.

33. Nathan Wright, ed., *What Black Educators Are Saying* (New York: Hawthorn Books, 1970); *Education and Black Struggle;* Alan A. Altschuler, *Community Control: The Black Demand for Participation in Large American Cities* (New York: Pegasus, 1970).

34. Slaughter, "Alienation of Afro-American Children," p. 144.

35. Novak, "One Species, Many Cultures," p. 120.

36. Odis Rhodes, "Some Implications for Teaching Reading to Speakers of Black Dialect" (unpublished manuscript, Stephen F. Austin State University, 1972).

37. Christopher Jencks et al., *Inequality: A Reassessment of the Effect of Family and Schooling* (New York: Basic Books, 1972); Samuel Bowles and Herbert Gintis, *Schooling in Capitalist America: Educational Reform and the Contradictions of Economic Life* (New York: Basic Books, 1975); A. H. Raskin, "The Changing Face of the Labor Force," *New York Times,* Feb. 15, 1976, p. 4 E.

38. Harold Cruse, *The Crisis of the Negro Intellectual* (New York: William Morrow, 1967), p. 108.

39. Frank Kofsky, *Black Nationalism and the Revolution in Music* (New York: Pathfinder Press, 1970), p. 10.

40. Edsel Erickson, Clifford Bryan, and Lewis Walker, eds., *Social Change, Conflict, and Education* (Columbus, Ohio: Charles E. Merrill, 1972), p. 455.

41. Valentine, "Deficit, Difference, and Bicultural Models of Afro-American Behavior," p. 10.

42. Valentine, "Deficit, Difference, and Bicultural Models of Afro-American Behavior," p. 8.

43. The idea of a separate Afro-American culture has not been defended in this paper, but it has been developed elsewhere by scores of scholars. A few are listed here: John W. Blassingame, *The Slave Community: Plantation Life in the Antebellum South* (New York: Oxford University Press, 1972); Peter H. Wood, *Black Majority: Negroes in Colonial South Carolina from 1670 through the Stono Rebellion* (New York: Alfred A. Knopf, 1974); Eugene D. Genovese, *Roll, Jordan, Roll: The World the Slaves Made* (New York: Pantheon Books, 1974); Herbert G. Gutman, *The Black Family in*

Slavery and Freedom, 1750-1925 (New York: Pantheon Books, 1976); Lawrence W. Levine, *Black Culture and Black Consciousness: Afro-American Thought from Slavery to Freedom* (New York: Oxford University Press, 1977); Leroi Jones, *Blues Peoples: The Negro Experience in White America and the Music That Developed from It* (New York: Praeger, 1972); Eileen Southern, *The Music of Black Americans: A History* (New York: W. W. Norton, 1971); Sterling D. Brown, *Negro Poetry and Drama and the Negro in American Fiction* (New York: Atheneum, 1937); Leonard E. Barett, *Soul Force: African Heritage in Afro-American Religion* (New York: Anchor Books, 1974); Harold Cruse, *The Crisis of the Negro Intellectual* (New York: William Morrow, 1967); John Lovell, Jr., *Black Song: The Forge and the Flame: The Story of How the Afro-American Spiritual Was Hammered Out* (New York: Macmillan, 1972); Addison Gayle, Jr., ed., *The Black Aesthetic* (New York: Doubleday, 1972); George Kent, *Blackness and the Adventure of Western Culture* (Chicago: Third World Press, 1972).

44. Nathan Glazer, *Affirmative Discrimination: Ethnic Inequality and Public Policy* (New York: Basic Books, 1975), pp. 22-27.

45. Eugene D. Genovese, *In Red and Black: Marxian Explorations in Southern and Afro-American History* (New York: Pantheon Books, 1971), pp. 33-34; Carl Degler, "Slavery and the Genesis of American Race Prejudice," *Comparative Studies in Society and History,* vol. 2 (Oct., 1959); Winthrop D. Jordan, *White over Black: American Attitudes toward the Negro, 1550-1812* (Chapel Hill: University of North Carolina Press, 1968); David B. Davis, *The Problem of Slavery in Western Culture* (Ithaca, N.Y.: Cornell University Press, 1966); Charles H. Lyons, *To Wash an Aethiop White: British Ideas about Black African Educability 1530-1960* (New York: Teachers College Press, 1975).

46. Glazer, *Affirmative Discrimination,* pp. 177, 185, 187-88.

47. Sheldon S. Wolin, "The New Conservatives," *New York Review of Books,* Feb. 5, 1976, pp. 6-11; Irving Kirstol, "What is a 'Neo-Conservative'?," *Newsweek,* Jan. 19, 1976, p. 17.

48. Albert N. Keim, ed., *Compulsory Education and the Amish: The Right Not To Be Modern* (Boston: Beacon Press, 1975), p. 116.

49. Many of the ideas in the last two paragraphs were argued in the cases presented in Keim, *Compulsory Education and the Amish.*

VIRGINIA HELD

Men, Women, and Equal Liberty

I

Human beings have rights to liberty, and human beings have rights to equality. If we combine what the principles providing these rights require (though not all principles combine this way), we can conclude that we have rights to equal liberty. However, an examination of any contemporary society will show that such rights are systematically denied to many persons.

An examination of our conceptions of liberty may indicate that a faulty conception of liberty has significantly contributed to the denial of equal liberty to many persons. I shall argue that this is so. I shall in what follows use the terms 'liberty' and 'freedom' interchangeably, as do most writers. Although there may be reasons for moving toward distinguishing 'liberty' and 'freedom,' usage has not yet sorted them out sufficiently to make doing so other than a stipulation which I shall at this time refrain from making.

Were one to develop such a distinction, it would suggest, I think, that liberty is a part of freedom, that part to which we have rights which ought to be guaranteed by law. Liberty is something the law could assure us, though it often fails now to do so. Liberty is something we have or don't have, depending on law and its effectiveness. Freedom, in contrast, is something we can go on having more and more of. Law can assure part of it, but freedom as the creative development of the self and the society goes far beyond what law can provide. But as I say, in *this* paper, I shall use the terms interchangeably without trying to make a distinction.

The idea that a right to liberty is a right to be left alone, not interfered with, not forcibly coerced, has a long and familiar history. In the seventeenth century, Hobbes provided, as he so often did, a classic formulation: "Liberty, or Freedome," he wrote, "signifieth (properly) the absence of Opposition; (by Opposition I mean externall Impediments of motion). . . . "[1] Thus, for Hobbes, we are free to walk down the road if no one interferes with us, if no one subjects us to external impediments, and if no law forbids it. Locke has been interpreted as having a similar conception of liberty, although I think there is room for argument about this. In any case, the conception of freedom as the absence of interference has become a rather standard part of the western liberal tradition, at least in its theoretical formulations, if less so in some of its more recent practices.

The assumption underlying this conception was that a man left alone could fend for himself. He could till the soil or ply a trade and make a living. If he had no soil or trade, he could go off into unoccupied territory somewhere and begin. (Locke suggested that he could always go to America.) If others would only not interfere and force him to do things he did not want to do, he would be able to live his life, earn a living, acquire some property, and be his own man. Of course some liberty would have to be yielded—people would not be free from legal restraint to murder and steal, for instance—but only for the sake of the superior liberty which would ensue as people were left alone, free from attack, to live their lives in civil peace and safety.

How limited this assumption was can be seen immediately if one includes women within the picture. A woman was never imagined to be able in a comparable sense to fend for herself and was never permitted the chance. She could only attach herself to a man from whom she might, if lucky, receive decent treatment in exchange for total dependence. If merely left alone, she and her children would be helpless. A man could choose to take on a family to provide for or not. A woman could not choose to be a "free man" in the sense provided by this conception of freedom. Her only choice, and even that was rarely granted, was on whom she would be dependent, and by whom she would be dominated. But because it was to such a large extent *mere women* (though also servants) for whom this kind of liberty could provide so little freedom, the unsatisfactoriness of the concept was easily ignored. Liberty for women was not even a pious hope.

The conception of freedom as the right to be left alone remains unsatisfactory, however, for all those not favored by current economic, social, political, and legal arrangements. The assumption that a person not interfered with can adequately acquire what he or she needs to live is obviously false in a modern society where we find ourselves with an earth and an industrialized economy which are already fully appropriated, and which others often have no willingness at all to make available in any way to us. The traditional conception of freedom serves to camouflage the degree to which some persons are favored by the status quo and others denied the chance to be free. It allows those who already have privileges and property to hang on to them without interference, while preventing those who lack such privileges and property from acquiring them. It allows those who call themselves libertarians to claim to be concerned with enlarging freedom when in fact they are concerned with enlarging the economic privileges of those whom their favored economic arrangements would allow to be overprivileged. And it allows those who call themselves liberals to be irresponsibly unaware of the extent to which their policies fail to work toward greater freedom for those disadvantaged by current arrangements: for women, for the members of minorities, for the poor, the sick, the unemployed, for the young and old.

The conception of freedom standard in the western liberal tradition deriving from Hobbes and Locke is often described as "negative freedom." The distinction between negative and positive freedom was made familiar by Isaiah Berlin in his essay "Two Concepts of Liberty," published in 1958.[2] Negative liberty or freedom is freedom *from:* freedom from interference, from being pushed around, restricted, locked up.

We are free in the negative sense if we are free *from* being arrested for speaking our minds, being attacked as we walk in the street, being forcibly prevented from meeting with others. Positive

68

freedom, in contrast, is being free *to do* various things. As Isaiah Berlin interprets it, basing his view of positive freedom on the Hegelian and Idealist tradition rather than the tradition of Hobbes and Locke, we are free in the positive sense when we are guided by our better, rational selves, not led by our passions, free *to do* what we ought to do. We are, for instance, free to serve the common interest when we overcome our selfishness and take part in a community project.

Berlin discusses the dangers of the positive conception of freedom: it leads to the view that we give people freedom by making them do what they ought to do. If, for instance, we prohibit the drinking of alcohol, people will be free to choose soberly and act rationally, hence the prohibition of alcohol might not be seen as an interference with freedom. Berlin would insist that we be able to say that prohibiting people from, say, drinking alcohol *is* a restriction on freedom. Then we can consider whether such an interference with freedom is or is not justifiable, or worth it, in terms of other considerations, such as health. But we must first be able to recognize it for what it is: a loss of freedom.

Recognizing the dangers to which a positive conception of freedom has often led, from Rousseau onwards, Berlin argues for the negative conception as the more satisfactory and more basic.[3] But, it can be argued, his formulations of negative and positive freedom may be misleading. He seems to set up a disparity between the contexts for negative and positive freedom such that negative freedom has to do primarily with *physical* impediments and interferences to action, and positive freedom with essentially *mental* aspects of willing and rationality and morality. However, in contrast with Berlin's two contexts, if we try to give as fair an account as we can of these matters we seem to be able to make good sense of negative and positive freedom in both the physical, material sense, and in the mental, rational sense. And it seems an unfair formulation to see negative freedom as physical and material, positive freedom as mental and rational, despite the fact that the traditions in which the two conceptions have developed have had these different emphases.

For instance, we can be free *from* physical assault as we sit in the park and free *to* eat a lunch while we are there. The former requires that police protection against assault be provided by the society; the latter that the society has provided a park and made it possible for us to acquire food. Or, we can be free *from* our urge to watch inane entertainment on TV and free *to* follow the intellectual interest of our better selves. The former requires that our will resist an impulse, the latter that it freely choose a goal to pursue.

Freedom in the rational, willing sense involves the question of free and rational choice at the mental, psychological level, and it seems to be a different sort of freedom than the kind having to do with action and the material, physical hindrances to it or incapacities for it. Social arrangements may facilitate or hamper both kinds of freedom, but these two kinds of freedom seem distinct quite apart from the negative/positive distinction. If we agree with this, we would have to recognize four kinds of freedom: negative-physical, positive-physical, negative-mental, and positive-mental.

A much more satisfactory conception than this multiplication of categories may be that offered by Gerald MacCallum in his article called "Negative and Positive Freedom," published in 1967. Freedom, he argues, is always a triadic relation: *We are free from x to do y.* He writes, "Whenever the freedom of some agents is in question, it is always freedom from some constraint or restriction on, interference with, or barrier to doing, not doing, becoming, or not becoming something. Such freedom is thus always *of* something (an agent or agents), *from* something, *to* do, not do, become or not become something; it is a triadic relation."[4] *All* cases of freedom, he thinks, can be fitted into this format. Disputes will be over what can be substituted for the x's and y's.

To take our previous examples: we can be free *from* assault *to* eat lunch in the park; we can be free *from* the impulse to watch TV *to* concentrate on more worthwhile pursuits. And so on. But not everything can count as a limitation or enlargement of freedom. We should not, for instance, substitute for x conditions over which human beings can have no control, or for y actions beyond the range of possible human action. It would not be helpful, for instance, to say we are not *free* from the tendency to fall if we walk off a high ledge, or that we are not *free* to live to be 1,000 years old. Of course we cannot escape the laws of nature and do these things. But they are not limitations of *freedom* in the sense in which we are concerned with it when we speak of rights to freedom. We should restrict the application of terms such as 'freedom' and 'coercion' to what results from the actions of other people, not natural events, and to humanly possible actions. Thus, if a person lacks shelter because of an earthquake, this does not deprive him of freedom. However, if others prevent him from entering intact buildings, or fail to come to his aid by sharing their surplus shelter with him, this may well do so.

An alternative view to Gerald MacCallum's is to maintain the concept of liberty as the absence of external impediments, but to include within the notion of impediments the lack of access to what we need to be free. This is the approach of C. B. Macpherson. He writes, "Liberty is the absence of humanly imposed impediments . . . these impediments include not only coercion of one individual by another, and direct interference with individual activities by the state or society (beyond what is needed to secure each from invasion by others), but also lack of equal access to the means of life and the means of labour."[5] This would mean including within the notion of negative liberty the lack of a capacity to do various things when this lack results from the actions of other human beings, as when people retain and laws protect property in such a way that others are denied access to what they need.

I think the arguments in favor of MacCallum's approach are stronger, since it often seems strained to think of absences as the kinds of impediments we want to be free *from*. It is not strange, however, to think of such absences as limiting freedom, and Mac-Callum's format allows us to say this. Thus we could say that we are not free *from* a certain legal impediment maintaining another's property *to* occupy an empty building and obtain shelter.

Stanley Benn and W. L. Weinstein, in their article "Being Free to Act, and Being a Free Man" (which I regret is not called "Being Free to Act, and Being a Free Person," since I share so many of the positions in it), accept MacCallum's basic format. They agree with the linking of freedom from and freedom to do, and try to go on to characterize the sorts of things we can be free from and free to do.

They argue that the conditions of unfreedom "restrict choice by making alternatives unavailable or ineligible."[6] For instance, the person threatened with death if he does not raise his hands over his head is rendered unfree by having the choice of not raising his hands made ineligible. Similarly, the worker who has to sell his labor for an exploitative wage or face starvation is also rendered unfree because the choice not to sell it is not really open to him. Benn and Weinstein hold, as I have elsewhere argued, that such denials of liberty can occur through offers which persons in need cannot resist as well as through threats to make their lives worse than they are already.[7] Thus a person in very great need may be unfree to turn down an offer as well as unfree to resist a threat. Benn and Weinstein agree that to interpret freedom as negative freedom only is mistaken.

II

Sometimes it is suggested that the acquisition of what one needs to live and be free should be considered an aspect of welfare, not freedom. I shall argue that this is not an adequate solution to the problem. To be concerned with equal freedom we must include among the aspects of freedom the acquisition of the means to be free as well as the maintenance of such means by those who already have them. Otherwise, concern for rights to freedom will unfairly profit those who benefit already from the status quo.

Certainly our welfare and the general welfare are values in which we all have interests, but welfare is different from freedom. Sometimes our interests in welfare and efficiency must be weighed against our rights to freedom when the two conflict, and sacrifices of one or the other may be necessary. But the tradition which limits freedom to the right to be left alone cannot adequately take into account the *rights* to freedom (and not only the interests in welfare) of those who do not already have the means to be free. To be free, the man of property may need only to be free from interference, but the person without property and the means to acquire it needs more to be free than to be left alone with nothing.

It may be helpful to think of freedom in terms of independence, a much wider notion than the freedom from interference of standard negative freedom, and yet one traditionally associated with freedom in a way in which the components of welfare are not. It is then clear that for human beings to be independent in a developed, industrial society, and for independence to extend to groups previously excluded from it such as women, minorities, and the poor, human beings must be assured of much more than an absence of interference. They must be assured of access to the means to live: decent jobs, minimum incomes, medical care, housing they can afford, child care for their children. Such provisions should not be imposed on people, but made available for them to choose.

A woman, for instance, cannot be free and independent if she is at the mercy of a man who can give or withhold the sustenance she needs to live. A worker cannot be free and independent if he is at the mercy of an employer who can give or withhold the job without which he would be destitute. What will contribute to their being free and independent is assurance of the necessary minimum of what they need to live, in the form of a guaranteed income or a right to a decent job. And these are just as essential for freedom and independence as the police protection traditionally associated with assuring freedom from attack, the negative freedom of noninterference.

Whether persons *feel* themselves to be independent or not is a somewhat different question. The capacities for self-deception are great and often widespread: employees of corporations imagine themselves independent because they can leave one job and find another equally damaging to their freedom; technicians and intellectuals imagine themselves at liberty because they don't acknowledge that the institutions which pay their salaries only do so to serve their own interests, and can cease doing so at will; women imagine themselves free because their husbands are generous or famous. But self-deception is at least challenged in times of high unemployment, institutional cutting back, and marital tension.

Of course we cannot all be independent of one another. We need each other economically, politically, emotionally. And we should not try to do without the benefits that can often be gained by mutual dependence among equals. But there now exist enormous differences in the degree of independence some of us are privileged to enjoy and others of us are systematically denied. To suppose that those privileged and those deprived in terms of such independence both enjoy equal liberty because both enjoy rights to free speech, to vote without interference, to be left alone, is ludicrous. To assure that persons in contemporary society truly have equal liberty we cannot interpret liberty only in the traditional negative sense but must enlarge it to include the freedom to live, to work, and to develop.

Despite the distorted picture it presents, the negative conception of freedom continues to exercise enormous influence. It underlies, for instance, a whole area of legal decisions in which the equal protection clause of the constitution is applied to certain legal freedoms but not to any kind of economic independence. The constitution requires in the Fourteenth Amendment "equal protection of the laws." This has led to Supreme Court decisions that find various interferences unconstitutional—for instance, a poll tax restricting voting, the statutory exclusion of blacks from juries, the exclusion of aliens from the bar, and the compulsory sterilization of habitual criminals—but the Supreme Court has not interpreted the constitutional provision as requiring any sort of equal protection to what persons need to live or develop. A California court had ruled that the financing of public school education through local taxation *was* in conflict with the equal protection provision, since poor districts were unable to provide educational opportunities to their children comparable to those provided by rich districts, but the Supreme Court, in another case, disagreed. The Supreme Court does not interpret the provision of equal protection as protection of our rights to be equally free to acquire even the essentials of what we need to live. It allows unequal school financing, unequal welfare benefits, grossly unequal housing and public services, and wildly unequal incomes, all supported to a large extent and in various ways by "the laws." The Supreme Court has for many years had a double standard, applying the constitutional provisions of due process and equal protection to certain personal rights but not to economic rights, which are seen essentially in terms of the unsatisfactory negative sense of freedom. As one writer states, "by virtue of the application of the double standard, the Court has for the past generation abdicated any constructive role in resolving this major issue of our time, the relationship between economic independence and individual freedom."[8]

And Congress has of course not yet recognized the rights of citizens to jobs, to a minimum income, to a basic minimum of necessities such as food or health care or housing which would allow citizens the beginnings of independence. When governmental assistance is sporadically, tentatively, and grudgingly provided, it is thought to be the result of governmental generosity, or largesse, not a recognition of citizens' rights. This failure should be recognized for what it is: a denial of the rights to equal freedom of large numbers of citizens.

III

The negative conception of freedom is also reflected in the works of the two most widely discussed and influential contemporary political philosophers, John Rawls and Robert Nozick. Though they differ very fundamentally in their conceptions of justice, their conceptions of freedom are not far apart, and this may render their theories somewhat less distant from one another than many critics have seemed to notice.

In *A Theory of Justice* Rawls seeks to formulate the fundamental principles which should guide the ordering of societies. He interprets social justice in terms of two principles which he thinks human beings would choose from a hypothetical original position—his version of the state of nature of classical theory. In this position people would all be equal and they would not know what particular characteristics they would have in any actual society. Not knowing if they would be white or black, male or female, talented or untalented, rich or poor, they would choose, impartially, principles that they would be willing to have social arrangements based upon, whether they themselves turned out to be advantaged or disadvantaged and no matter what position they would in fact come to occupy in actual society.

The principles Rawls thinks people would choose under such conditions are the following: (1) each person is to have an equal right to the most extensive basic liberty compatible with a similar liberty for others; (2) social and economic inequalities are to be arranged so that they are both (a) to the greatest benefit of the least advantaged and (b) attached to offices and positions open to all under conditions of fair equality of opportunity.[9] These principles, Rawls argues, would be arranged in such a way that the first, requiring equal liberty, always took priority over the second, concerning the distribution of wealth and power.

The second principle, as has been widely observed, would seem to have quite radical implications. It would justify a social arrangement providing a disparity in income—for instance, one in which the managers of corporations earn large sums and the workers for these corporations small sums—only if such an arrangement benefited the least advantaged, by increasing total production, say, and making workers better off than if both managers and workers earned equal amounts. Taking this principle seriously would certainly require an absolutely tremendous overhaul of contemporary social institutions, since it cannot possibly be argued that the vast disparities in power and possessions that now exist between rich white males and everyone else work out to the advantage of the least advantaged.

However, the radical implications of this principle are seriously undercut by Rawls's conception of freedom in the first principle, which always takes priority. The second principle is not to come into effect until the requirements of the first principle are satisfied, and the first principle requires equal liberty in what amounts to a traditional, negative sense only. Although Rawls's formulation accords with MacCallum's triadic one, he does not count deprivations—such as a lack of money or an inability to find a job or a lack of political influence, even when these lacks are brought about by the actions of others—among the interferences which liberty is to free us from. Nor will liberty in his view provide the capacities to gain food, income, education, etc., to those without them. Rawls distinguishes between liberty and the worth of liberty—the poor person may be free from interference, but his freedom may be worth little to him because he cannot do much with it. It is only liberty, as distinct from the worth of liberty, however, that is called for by the first principle.[10] Thus the first principle may require equal liberty from interference for the rich to stay rich and powerful and for the poor to stay poor and powerless. This kind of equal liberty, Rawls holds, must be assured before the second principle, requiring distribution of the worth of liberty in such a way as to improve the lot of the disadvantaged, is applied.

Many judgments thought implicit in Rawls's theory may in this way be deflected, and freedom of a kind that will have worth to the poor and powerless, the female and non-white and unlucky, does not seem to be adequately provided for in Rawls's theory once the meaning of liberty is unveiled.

In Robert Nozick's "entitlement theory of justice" the unfortunate implications of the negative conception of freedom are positively glaring. In his recent highly praised and widely noted book, *Anarchy, State, and Utopia,* Nozick considers how something equivalent to state power might justifiably arise in a hypothetical state of nature without infringing on anyone's rights and without coercing anyone. Nozick claims to be trying to assure above all our rights to freedom. He does not claim to be arguing for equal freedom, since equality is for him only something governments can impose on people, not something to which we have moral rights. He does claim to be defining rights which should not be infringed, which are not to be sacrificed for other objectives, and which include our rights to freedom. The only kind of freedom he considers, however, is the standard negative freedom from interference.

For Nozick, economic arrangements are prior to political and legal ones. His hypothetical state of nature would come equipped, remarkably, with a "market" and "money," with "companies," "contracts," "clients," and "customers," and with property rights to the exclusive and permanent possession of things. In this state of nature, some people would acquire much property and some very little, and people would buy protection of their rights. Eventually one of the protection agencies supplying this service would become dominant, as it acquired the most customers, and thus, in Nozick's view, something equivalent to a state could be born.

For Nozick, economic transactions are never coercive. If a poor person sells his lifetime labor for a pittance, even if he sells himself into slavery to stay alive, he has in Nozick's view made a free choice to do so. As long as the rich man buying up the poor person's life or labor does not threaten to make the poor person's life worse than it already is if he does not sell, such buying up of the lives of others is not, in Nozick's view, an infringement on anyone's freedom. For Nozick, if we leave people alone we respect their rights, even if they are starving and we refuse to share with them any of our surplus.

Unlike Locke, whom he likes to claim as his philosophical ancestor, Nozick does not recognize the rights of anyone to have others, no matter how wealthy and powerful these others are, share with him anything of what he needs to live and to develop. Locke had written that "God . . . has given no one of his children such a property, in his peculiar portion of the things of this world, but that he has given his needy brother *a right* to the surplusage of his goods; so charity gives *every man a title* to so much out of another's plenty, as will keep him from extreme want."[11] Locke recognized full well the coercive possibilities of economic power. He warned, "A man can no more justly make use of another's necessity, to force him to become his vassal, by withholding that relief God requires him to afford to the wants of his brother, than he that has more strength can seize upon a weaker, master him to his obedience, and with a dagger at his throat offer him death or slavery."[12]

For Nozick, freedom for the rich and powerful requires that they be free from interference in hanging on to their holdings. An interference such as taxation to provide for those in need is in Nozick's view an unjustified attack on their freedom: "taxation of earnings from labor is on a par with forced labor."[13] The poor and powerless will likewise be free from attack and from having their holdings taken away. But if they have no holdings, if they lack what they need to live, they are left with the freedom to nothing. The deficiencies of a purely negative conception of freedom have seldom been more striking than in Nozick's depiction of what he takes to be a free society, where some persons will be free to sell themselves into slavery in exchange for food and others will be free to buy them.

A further consequence of the negative conception of freedom is the direction it suggests for appropriate government action. Again

Nozick's discussion illustrates the problem. Given his view of freedom, not only is that government best which governs least, but the *only* functions of government which are justified are those of the traditional night-watchman state, protecting citizens against murder, assault, theft, and fraud.[14] These are the functions of government which protect negative freedom. They suit the interests of those with ample property and power, protecting the fortunate from losing what they have. They do little for those who lack what they need to live and grow, who have not been able to acquire even basic necessities. To be protected against attack when one is already dying of avoidable hunger or disease is hardly to be a free person.

This emphasis on the night-watchman functions of government leads, according to Nozick, to a minimal government. But it may instead and as easily lead to a police state in which vast resources are devoted to preventing those in desperate need from acting to improve their situation. If no other chance to avoid extreme deprivation is open to a person except taking what he needs, he will doubtless be inclined toward such action. Nozick's theory justifies the use of the power of government to prevent him from, and punish him for, theft, but it does not justify the use of the power of government to provide him with what he needs to live, by, for instance, providing him with a job. So the supposedly minimal state favored by Nozick could well develop into a vast police apparatus protecting the privileged few from the hungry and desperate. It would certainly encourage the development of a comparable situation on a world scale, with the rich nations spending ever-greater proportions of their resources to arm themselves against the poor, guarding their hoarded wealth while deprivation raged ever more frightfully elsewhere. A state which would concern itself with the needs of the hungry and desperate might be far more minimal than would Nozick's night-watchman state in terms of numbers employed, expenses, and obtrusiveness. And it might go far further in assuring our rights to freedom in a full and satisfactory sense.[15]

As recently as 1971 the U.S. Supreme Court characterized welfare payments as "charity." Thus a woman who expends her labor taking care of small children, but is not paid by anyone for this labor, nor even given an allowance by a husband on whom she is dependent, is thought to be receiving charity in merely being accorded the freedom to eat and be sheltered. Similarly, much popular sentiment regards the provision or subsidization of services by government as an unnecessary gift to those who, it is thought, should instead provide for their own needs, such as for decent and paid work, for medical care, for housing, for transportation. But to regard the night-watchman functions of government as legitimate, and the provision of the means to live as not legitimate, is merely a reflection of a traditional but unsatisfactory negative conception of freedom and our rights to it.

Of course the arrangements we now have do not by any means embody the ideals of negative freedom, of the night-watchman state. Our government now provides enormous subsidies for powerful corporations and wealthy individuals through tax benefits and expenditures for defense, highway construction, housing mortgages, etc. But the reforms sought by many of those who claim to be the champions of freedom aim only at the no less unsatisfactory night-watchman model of government.

Were we to take freedom really seriously, we would reorganize the structures of work so that production would be aimed at enlarging human freedom rather than maximizing profits and so that democratic self-determination would be extended into the organization of economic life. We would see to it that the activity of work would become as much as possible the source for everyone of free and creative expression, for we express our lives in our work as we express our thoughts in our speech, and for both we need freedom. But I have emphasized in this paper a much more modest advance—the assurance of only the most basic necessities without which we cannot have liberty. If the priority of liberty is maintained, or if a commitment to freedom is taken to be the primary source of our rights, then liberty must be understood to include rights to what we need to live and to be free whether we are already economically self-sufficient or whether we are not.

In sum, there is no more a moral right to be free to hang on to what one already has than there is a moral right to be free to help oneself to what one needs. Both sorts of rights have to be developed with a view to the rights of others, and a proper concern for our rights to equal liberty requires an appreciation of and respect for both aspects of freedom.

REFERENCES

1. Hobbes, *Leviathan,* chap. 21.
2. See Isaiah Berlin, *Four Essays on Liberty* (London: Oxford University Press, 1969).
3. See Berlin, *Four Essays,* p. 171, but also the note on p. lviii.
4. Gerald MacCallum, "Negative and Positive Freedom," *The Philosophical Review,* vol. 76 (July, 1967), p. 314. See also Felix Oppenheim, *Dimensions of Freedom* (New York: St. Martin's, 1961).
5. C. B. Macpherson, *Democratic Theory* (London: Oxford University Press, 1973), p. 96.
6. S. I. Benn and W. L. Weinstein, "Being Free to Act and Being a Free Man," *Mind,* vol. 80 (Apr., 1971), p. 197.
7. See Virginia Held, "Coercion and Coercive Offers," in J. R. Pennock and J. W. Chapman, eds., *Coercion, Nomos,* vol. 14 (New York: Aldine-Atherton, 1972).
8. Richard Funston, "The Double Standard of Constitutional Protection in the Era of the Welfare State," *Political Science Quarterly,* vol. 90 (Summer, 1975), p. 286.
9. John Rawls, *A Theory of Justice* (Cambridge: Harvard University Press, 1971), pp. 60, 83, 302.
10. In Rawls's words: "The inability to take advantage of one's rights and opportunities as a result of poverty and ignorance, and a lack of means generally, is sometimes counted among the constraints definitive of liberty. I shall not, however, say this, but rather I shall think of these things as affecting the worth of liberty, the value to individuals of the rights that the first principle defines." (p. 204). On this issue see Norman Daniels, "Equal Liberty and Unequal Worth of Liberty," in N. Daniels, ed., *Reading Rawls* (New York: Basic Books, 1975).
11. Locke, *The First Treatise of Government,* par. 42.
12. Locke, *First Treatise,* par. 42.
13. Robert Nozick, *Anarchy, State, and Utopia* (New York: Basic Books, 1974), p. 169.
14. Nozick, *Anarchy, State, and Utopia,* p. 162*n.*
15. For further discussion of Nozick, see Virginia Held, "John Locke on Robert Nozick," *Social Research,* vol. 43 (Spring, 1976).

MIHAILO MARKOVIĆ

The Relationship between Equality
and Local Autonomy

All great ideas appear at first in very general abstract form, challenging only in thought the existing forms of human life. Then,
slowly, as opportunities for their practical implementation arise,
they become more particular, emphasizing just that dimension of
the general problem which allows practical solution in the given
historical situation. Often such a particular interpretation is replaced by another, opposite, one, equally particular and one-sided.
However, this confrontation eventually opens up the possibility of
developing a much richer, much more concrete and synthetic concept which reasserts the initial universal in the full wealth of its
particular historical dimensions and its links with other universal
ideas of the given epoch. Whenever we deal with a definite practical
problem—as in our case the equality which is possible in an autonomous particular community—we tend to be methodically one-sided,
and our solutions tend to be limited. However, we shall be aware of
this one-sidedness and of the limitations of our practical solutions
only if we never give up the power of critical thinking. This critical and self-critical rational power stems precisely from a fully developed theoretical framework of universal ideas about the given
historical epoch.

The problem of equality was first posed in ancient culture in its
most abstract, religious, and philosophical form as equality of an
individual *as a human being* in general. By the end of ancient
civilization and in the modern bourgeois state political and legal
discussions were brought into focus, and equality was seen as primarily equality of an individual *as a citizen,* as a member of politi-

cal society. In recent times equality is also treated as an economic, social, cultural, educational problem; it becomes more and more the problem of the individual *as a member of a concrete working and living community*.

In all great ancient religions, men were treated as equals in some important aspects. Hinduism, while justifying the extreme social inequalities of a caste system, taught that all persons are equally capable of self-discovery, self-perfection, and becoming the center of the highest religious experience. In the same way, from the Buddhist point of view each man can reach the incomparable security of Nirvana if he perceives and overcomes the wretchedness of what is subject to birth, old age, disease, and death, to sorrow and corruption. Judaism and Christianity claimed that all men are equal in the sense that they all were created by God, have equal souls, the inner image of their divine creator, and are equally responsible to Him. Apostle Paul says to the Galatians: "There is no such thing as Jew and Greek, slave and free man, male and female; for you are all one person in Christ Jesus." In the Bible one finds already the idea of universal equality before the law, divine law to be sure: "Ye shall have one law for the stranger and citizen alike for I, the Lord, am your God."

In its secular, rational form the idea of equality appears for the first time in the views of the Sophists. For example, Antiphon considers that "our natural endowment is the same for us all on all points, whether we are Greeks or barbarians. Therefore, it is barbarian to revere and venerate one only because he was born of a great house." After these first indications we find a consistent doctrine of universal *natural equality* in the philosophy of Stoa. Over a long period of time the Stoics argued, in opposition to Plato and Aristotle, that all men are alike by nature because they all possess rationality and the ability to know and do the good. Cicero in *De Legibus* said that if bad habits and false beliefs did not twist the weaker minds and turn them in whatever direction they were inclined, no one would be so like his own self as all men would be like all others.

At a time of enormous social inequalities the idea of a universal natural equality must have appeared rather unrealistic, but its authors did not claim to be giving descriptions of social realities.

They projected natural equality into the past, into an early age of innocence preceding the introduction of property, slavery, and the state. Or they completely internalized equality and projected it into a subjective, spiritual, purely moral sphere of human activity. According to Seneca and Marcus Aurelius, even when the body of a slave was at the disposition of a master, he was still proclaimed equal in the sense that he was said to have an equally free mind, could live according to the reason of his own nature in spite of the most unfavorable circumstances, and could partake in the good and the virtuous, which was thought to be the same for all men.

This dualism—of the inner spiritual equality versus external social inequality, of the past equality versus the present inequality, of the natural state versus social and political organization, of potential human being versus actual distorted reality—has been characteristic of egalitarian humanist thought during the whole epoch of class society.

What characterizes the second stage in the history of the idea of equality are the political and legal applications of the idea of natural equality during an age of rapid material and cultural development. There is a long period of transition. The idea of natural equality was taken over by the Roman law; for example, in Justinian's *Institutes* we find the passage, "By the law of nature all men from the beginning were born free," and in the *Digest,* "according to natural law all men are equal."

From the Roman law the idea of natural equality was transmitted to medieval legal thought and from there to the Renaissance culture. Nicholas of Cusa was the first who derived very definite political implications from the idea in its abstract form. In his *De Concordantia Catholica* (1433) he said: "Accordingly since by nature all men are free, any authority . . . must come solely from the agreement and consent of the subjects. For if men are by nature equal in power and equally free, the properly ordered authority of one who is naturally equal in power can only be established by the choice and consent of the others and also law is constituted by consent."

In subsequent centuries, in classical liberalism and the Enlightenment and in the democratic ideology of the great bourgeois revolutions in America and France, a powerful criticism of authoritarian and hierarchical features of feudal society was fully elaborated. The fiction of the social contract served not only as the explanation of the origin of the state authority but also as the justification of the people's sovereignity and of the inalienable rights of the citizen. Among these rights there were quite definite civil liberties: of thought, self-expression, organization, election, demonstration, public protest, etc. Equality before the law was guaranteed, and this was a very great step in the process of human emancipation—not only in comparison with feudal society but also with respect to those political inequalities which until this day have survived in all those present-day societies which did not have the benefits of the Enlightenment and of bourgeois democratic revolution. It is important to observe that the more radical thinkers of these revolutions far surpassed their limited historical task. Rousseau already saw the origin of the inequality of civil society in the emergence of private property. He said, in *Discourse,* "The first man who fenced in an area and said 'This is mine' and who found people simple enough to believe him was the real founder of civil society." Rousseau was also already aware of the dangers of political alienation: he observed that if a society was too big and kept a professional army, the representatives of the people would become alienated and true democracy would disappear. People can be sovereign only in smaller communities. It was Rousseau who first posed the problem with which we are presently dealing: Is it not the case that human equality can be achieved only within an autonomous community?

However, Rousseau was an exception. The prevalent liberalist political philosophy almost completely abstracted the political from the economic dimension of social life. Society was split into a political and a civil sphere. In the former, equality was reduced to the equality of civil rights, equality before the law; in the latter, to equality of opportunity. Today, however, enormous differences in the distribution of wealth make the idea of equality of opportunity devoid of any sense, a sheer ideological myth. Because of factual drastic inequality of condition, some individuals are able to fully enjoy their civil rights, but for others most of these rights remain abstract possibilities entirely outside practical reach.

Modern socialist thought, especially the theory of Karl Marx, has further developed the idea of equality, elaborating especially its economic dimension. It should be emphasized, however, that this thought cannot be classified as radical egalitarianism. Marx was quite well aware of the natural differences among individuals and of the fact that these will increase in importance when institutions that favor social discrimination and inequality disappear (see, for example, the section on money in *Economic and Philosophical Manuscripts*). Marx was very far from conceiving communism as a society in which all individuals would be equally paid and cultivate a uniform style of life. His conception of equality was focused on the demand to abolish class exploitation, that is, to abolish privately owned capital and wage labor, to replace commodity production by production for human needs, and to substitute conscious regulation of production for blind, market regulation. However, these economic objectives are only one dimension of a very broadly articulated vision of universal human emancipation involving the transcendence of the state, the establishment of a federation of the producers' councils, and the creation of all the material and cultural conditions needed for the full development of each individual.

Today we must recognize how far we are from the realization of this vision, even in those societies which moved through the initial steps of a socialist revolution. Some of Marx's basic goals have been completely distorted, especially his unfortunately stated idea of "dictatorship of the proletariat" and the idea of central planning. Others, like his critique of bureaucracy, his ideas of remuneration according to work, and his belief that the workers' state should be transformed into a federation of workers' councils, have been forgotten.

We shall not deal with the abuses and distortions that the theory of Marx has undergone in the hands of his less competent and less humanist-minded followers, but will instead concentrate on a problem that Marx himself largely neglected, one which has remained unsolved by both contemporary liberal and socialist scholars. The problem is that of equality and autonomy. It can be analyzed into the following three questions:

1. What is the modern interpretation of equality and autonomy from the point of view of a critical social theory?

2. Is equality in some sense a necessary condition of autonomy in either working communities or in living local communities?

3. Under what conditions does autonomy promote human equality and universal human emancipation?

A humanist-oriented critical social theory tends to recognize essential limitations in the existing social structures and to indicate practical steps for abolishing those limitations. From this point of view, the concrete manifestation of the aspiration to equality in our time is the demand to abolish some existing forms of inequality. Yet here some distinctions need to be made.

There are different types of inequality and only some of them should be regarded as essential limitations in our historical epoch. Two distinctions are important. First, there is a difference between inequalities in genetically conditioned natural capacities, talents, interests, etc., on the one hand, and inequalities in roles and life styles as a result of the process of socialization, on the other. Second, there is a difference between mere differentiation and stratification, i.e., between inequality in kind and inequality in rank. On the basis of these two criteria one gets the following four types of inequality:

1. differentiation on the basis of natural capacities
2. stratification on the basis of natural capacities
3. differentiation on the basis of social roles
4. stratification on the basis of social roles

In every society there will be differences among individuals in their abilities, character, gifts, etc. Uniformity imposed by a rigid egalitarianism is incompatible with the individual self-realization that remains the very basic objective of all humanist thought. However, many apparent natural differences are not solely the consequence of differences in inherited genetic dispositions but also result from the social conditions under which the growth of a young individual takes place. Therefore, many apparent natural differences of rank that seem to result from differences in intelligence, talent, creative imagination, etc., may be reduced by creating appropriate favorable conditions for the growth of each individual and by opening up possibilities for those who were initially handicapped to catch up later.

Some inequalities in status on the basis of different abilities are unavoidable. It is essential, however, that these inequalities not involve any form of domination or economic exploitation. In a democratic socialist society in which productive forces are socialized and the institutions of the state replaced by self-government, brighter, abler, stronger individuals with greater integrity will likely more often be elected as representatives of their communities in self-governing councils and assemblies. But they must not be able to stay in power and enjoy material and other privileges: it is essential that they rotate and that the esteem and respect they might enjoy while they perform as elected representatives not involve any form of subordination and uncritical surrender to authority on the part of the electorate.

In every modern society there will be differential social roles, different forms of socially necessary work. It is essential, however, that they do not involve any political or economic hierarchy; they must remain differences in kind. The clerk in the city administration, the teacher, the farmer, the white-collar worker, and the blue-collar worker will be different in many respects, but one should not be treated as superior to the other.

What remains to be abolished is the stratification on the basis of different social roles. Until now some roles have had a privileged status and have brought with them power, wealth, prestige, and glorification. Modern development has made some of these roles socially redundant (king, priest, private capitalist). Some of them have survived (professional politician, manager, policeman, army officer) and have become the source of new elites that concentrate enormous alienated power in their hands. That may happen even when all classes have been abolished. Any theory that tries to understand social inequalities only in terms of class differences fails to understand this phenomenon. This is part of the reason why many Marxists fail to give an adequate explanation of social stratification in socialist countries.

Consequently, a more refined conceptual apparatus is needed for the description and analysis of social stratification. A distinction is needed, for example, between class domination, political power, and status. Elite or political power is not the same as ruling class. Political power is not always, and simply, concentration of economic power. Otherwise it would be impossible to explain the emergence of such varied political forms as fascism, the New Deal in the United States, socialist tendencies in Scandinavian countries, and the rise of bureaucracy in socialist countries. The power of bureaucracy does not derive from property rights nor from a special position in the production process, but from a privileged position in the process of social decision making. It is at least theoretically clear how to prevent the emergence of class differences on the basis of a differentiation in social roles. It would be essential to strictly apply the principle of remuneration according to work and consequently to prevent anyone from appropriating any form of surplus value on the basis of his specific social role. In other words, land rent, profit, and bureaucratic privileges would have to be radically abolished. ("Radicalism" here does not preclude appropriate changes taking place within a reasonably long period of time and in a way compatible with human dignity.)

It is also theoretically conceivable to prevent the emergence of a hierarchy of power. It is essential to introduce democratic elections, recall, and vertical rotation for all functions and to prevent any professional division in the whole sphere of social policy making. This does not exclude the professional division of work in the technical implementation of adopted policies. However, the technical would certainly have to be subordinated to the political (in this case, to non-professional politics).

It is not clear, however, how to prevent the acquisition of high status and prestige for performing certain social roles exceptionally well. High status may lead to great influence and eventually to a lasting political power. Charismatic leaders have often turned into dictators not only because of personal ambition but also because of their extraordinarily high status among the masses of the population. The only preventive remedy is the cultivation of a critical attitude toward leaders and a constant watch over the observance of the democratic norms of the society. In that case the only remaining elite in the society would be the elite of spirit, of good taste, and of moral authority. Nevertheless, this form of inequality does not jeopardize human relationships, nor does it degrade anybody; it is beneficial rather than detrimental or dangerous for the society.

A comparable analysis of the problem of freedom leads to the conclusion that one of the very basic limitations of all existing forms of social life is the prevailing heteronomy of decision making and acting at both the personal and communal level. This heteronomy is complete when an external power orders the subject of decision making (a person, a working organization, or a local community) what to do and how, where, and when to do it. This situation can be described as a complete lack of freedom, as slavery.

Some authors consider having at least two alternatives as a necessary and sufficient condition of freedom. However, choice among alternatives surely is a necessary but not a sufficient condition of freedom. It may still involve several kinds of heteronomy:

1. The framework of alternatives among which to choose may be entirely determined by outside forces. There is obviously not much freedom in a situation in which the subject is not in the position to influence the determination of the framework of possibilities and to expand it beyond certain traditional and externally imposed boundaries.

2. The criterion of choice may be more or less heteronomous. A subject may be free to choose, but his freedom will be illusory if the set of values according to which the choice is made is not itself autonomously selected but rather is externally imposed in a process of authoritarian education, cultural manipulation, or ideological propaganda.

3. A number of modalities of choice may also be determined by an outside authority. There is not much freedom in a situation in which the subject has no say as to when, where, and how he will choose among given possibilities.

In order to illustrate these distinctions let us assume that the subject in question is a local community. In a very authoritarian, centralistic system heteronomy is almost complete. A detailed, rigid plan will decide what this particular community will produce, whether it will develop as an agricultural, industrial, or mining community, where it will get the necessary raw materials, how much of its production it will be obliged to deliver to the state and at what price, who will be its leaders, what will be taught in its schools, whether investments will be made to build a hospital, whether its citizens will be able to move to other communities, which information the local newspaper will be allowed to print, etc.

In a nonauthoritarian, reasonably decentralized society a community will be able to choose within a certain framework of possibilities. However, this need not bring much freedom. The community may be given two options, neither of which is satisfactory. There could be an election between two candidates neither of which is desirable. The community could be "allowed" to choose between two variants of a law, of a general plan of development, of a plan of production, or of a new education policy, but it could be that the community has in no way participated in the drafting of these alternatives. This kind of choice does not eliminate heteronomy and a sense of alienation—it only helps to avoid the greater evil.

Heteronomy of criteria consists of imposing on a community values with respect to which the choice will be made. Compulsion through brute force and threat of sanctions is replaced here by ideological manipulation and the force of tradition. Members of a community will feel free to choose among alternatives but may not be aware how much their choice is conditioned by the prevalent scale of values in the social system in which they live or by traditional views and preferences. In a liberal bourgeois society a community will systematically prefer its residents to solve their own problems, will favor private business, competition, and pluralism, and will cultivate communal spirit primarily though the nuclear family and the church. In a Soviet-type system members of a community will be urged to attend political meetings and to engage in public activities of economic and political character; they will be free to go to church but discouraged from doing so; unity, discipline, and readiness to subordinate private life to collective demands will be persistently emphasized. There are a number of problems which would be either at the center of attention or almost completely neglected due to different hierarchies of values in these two types of communities. One community would prefer to build roads, parking lots, gasoline stations, shopping centers, small private houses; the other one would tend to neglect most of these and would prefer to invest in public buses, street cars, trolley buses, trains, big apartment houses, children's day-care centers. It is true that these preferences within each community are also technologically determined: if there are few cars there will be little real need to build parking lots. The fact is, however, that technological preferences, too, are ideologically conditioned: the difference between the emphasis on automobiles and consumer-goods production in one case and an accelerated state-planned development of heavy industry in the other reflects the difference between two world outlooks and two different perceptions of needs.

In most cases heteronomy of criteria is closely linked with heteronomy of timing and other modal aspects of choice. Other possibilities are usually not entirely rejected but are systematically postponed or reduced in level and intensity.

Thus autonomy means not only freedom of decision making in all matters that are not of universal concern for the whole society, but also freedom from ideological indoctrination and uncritically adopted traditional creeds. More specifically, autonomy of a local community involves two basic things:

1. A distinction between those issues which are of particular concern to the community, and should entirely be decided by it, and those issues which are of general concern to the whole larger society to which the community belongs, and should be decided by dialogue and eventual agreement among elected representatives of all local communities.

2. Determination of the basic goals which a society tries to achieve and in the light of which choices among alternatives will be made should be the final result of a serious democratic debate, a struggle of opinions, mutual criticism, and an exchange of in-

formation. Each community will take part in this process of common-will building and will be responsible for the final result: a conscious formulation of a long-range policy of development of the whole society. This kind of normative consciousness is fundamentally different from either the established tradition or the official ideology. Tradition is to a large extent unconscious, irrational, conservative, past-oriented, never exposed to a genuine radical critique from the point of view of contemporary social needs. Ideology expresses and rationalizes the particular interests of a ruling elite and is never reached in a process of an open, democratic, critical debate but is imposed by indoctrination, pressure to conform, rewards in case of positive response, and, more or less, harsh punishment in case of resistance.

The autonomy just described presupposes some kind of equality.

Equality of rights of each citizen within a community and each community within global society is a necessary although not a sufficient condition of autonomy. If some citizens had more rights than others they could dominate the community. If some communities had more rights or were represented by a greater number of delegates than the others, they could dominate the global society. If some communities were dominated by ruling elites, their delegates would serve the interests of those elites rather than the interests of the people. Other communities would, then, at best have the possibility of challenging their mandate and disregarding their views; at worst, the whole social structure would become hierarchical and decision making heteronomous. To be sure, this situation can arise despite the presence of a doctrine of equality of rights if economic wealth and actual political power are unequally distributed.

An interesting ambiguous case of local autonomy is that of Yugoslav communes. These are local communities embracing several dozens of thousands of inhabitants, in most cases a provincial town with its agricultural environs. Each commune has its own assembly composed of relatively democratically elected representatives. The assembly passes general statutes and rules, accepts long-range plans of development, and makes decisions about the use of local resources, transportation, culture, education, health service, local mass media, recreation facilities, and natural environment. Formally, the only limits of local autonomy are set, on the one hand, by the laws and constitutional principles laid down at a higher level of social organization (in the national republic and the federation of six republics) and, on the other hand, by the rights of citizens and self-governing working organizations at the level of the commune.

From a purely legal point of view this solution is almost ideal. It seems as if the proper balance has been established between freedom of a particular local community, freedom of global society, and freedom of individual citizens and working organizations. However, a critical analysis of the economic and political structure reveals at least the following three essential limitations of freedom at each of these levels:

1. Communes are equal legally but very unequal economically and culturally. Poorer communes in underdeveloped regions of the country do not have much choice and have many difficulties obtaining bare necessities and especially supporting their educational and cultural institutions. They usually lack the means to build up adequate hospitals and roads and cannot even think about preserving and beautifying the environment. Part of this inequality and consequent constraint on positive freedom is being removed by federal aid to developing regions. A really socialist-humanist feature of this form of aid is that it is given without any strings attached and without humiliating bureaucratic control of the way the aid is to be spent. However, the aid is not sufficient to reduce the gap between the increasingly richer, freer communes and the poorer, relatively more limited ones.

2. Considerable power in a commune is concentrated in the hands of a small group of local professional political cadres, party functionaries, and executives in the permanent apparatus of the communal assembly; they are sometimes joined by the leading managers of the economic organizations. They both strongly influence decision making in the communal assembly and take the liberty to interpret and implement in their own way the decisions taken by the assembly. As a rule, their loyalty does not go to the people of the commune but to those on whom their status and career de-

pend, leaders in the republic and federation. Thus a good part of the apparent autonomy of the commune turns out to be hetero-nomical following of the line imposed from outside, from "above." When the local bureaucracy follows leaders who turn out to be losers in the factional struggle in the political heights (like "nation-alists" in 1971 and "liberals" in 1972) then it is mercilessly purged, and purges are usually too urgent to allow enough time to save even the appearance of an autonomous, democratic recall.

3. Self-governing institutions composed of democratically elected, rotatable, recallable nonprofessional representatives of communes and producers' collectives are missing at the level of global society. Basic decisions are made by the professional political cadres in the federation and the republics. Some of these decisions take the form of orders, others involve the formulation of options or the determi-nation of fundamental criteria of evaluation, and still others in-volve the specification of time, place, and other modalities. All these forms of heteronomy tend to erode the communal autonomy which looks so impressive in legal documents.

Yugoslav experience is very valuable because it shows his-torically possible steps beyond the levels of equality and autonomy reached by the middle of the 1960s. Among them are the following:

1. Granted that absolute equalization of economic and cultural conditions of various local communities is not realistic even in a democratic socialist society, a reasonable and feasible objective is a long-term policy of reducing the gap between the advanced and underdeveloped regions and communities. For this purpose the institution of the Federal Fund for the aid to developing regions is the optimal solution, but the fund must be large enough not only to stop but even to reverse the actual trend of increasing the gap.

2. Assemblies of the communes must reassert themselves as centers of public power; they could and should become *de facto* what they already are *de jure,* according to the laws and the consti-tution. The professional executives and administrators that are needed must be reduced to the role of "public servants," employees strictly responsible to the assembly and dismissable by it.

3. The most difficult step is obviously the transformation of the organs of the state in the federation and republics into the organs of self-government, which boils down to the gradual substitution

95

of representatives elected for a limited period of time and strictly responsible to their constituencies for permanent leading professional cadres. Present-day heteronomy would be substantially reduced and communal autonomy translated from paper into life to the extent to which the representatives of the communes really participate in determining national policy alongside the representatives of the working organizations.

In the preceding remarks it was clearly implied that the unqualified principle of local autonomy does not always promote equality and universal human emancipation. In an extremely decentralized system each community would have the right to pursue its particular interests without much concern about the interests of other communities. However, because too few issues would be solved for the system as a whole, the system would suffer from frictions and conflicts among its different parts. A low level of coordination would lead to considerable waste of energy, skill, and material resources. Overemphasis on local autonomy and disregard of equality would almost inevitably increase the differences, cleavages, and tensions among various local communities. The more this crude, one-sided, egoistic autonomy is found in a modern industrialized society, the more economic and social life resemble a laissez-faire model and the greater the gap between the developed and underdeveloped areas and communities. This is not a problem that only capitalist societies are confronted with. In present-day Chinese society, which is very centralistic in some respects, the principle of self-reliance is advocated for the development of agricultural communes. As a consequence, the differences between richer and poorer communes are growing and will obviously give rise to very serious inequalities in the not-too-distant future. The Chinese leaders are aware of this likelihood and foresee a possibility of intensified class struggle in coming decades.

Like extreme egoistic individualism, extreme communal particularism is not a viable goal for any civilized society. In reality, autonomy of one local community has to be reconciled with autonomy and growth of other communities, which means that a measure of rational coordination is necessary in all matters of general concern.

Conflicts of particular interests have to be resolved by negotiation, compromise, and eventual agreement among elected representatives of all communities.

The proper method of negotiation and agreement is a much more democratic procedure of decision making than traditional majority vote: the latter imposes the will of the larger part of society on the smaller one, the former consistently respects the autonomy of each part. However, the method of agreement is not free of all weaknesses, and two of them could be quite serious.

When the representatives of a community belong to a political party, then no matter how clearly defined the mandate of their constituency they could in the process of negotiation and searching for the compromise follow the will of their party and not the best interests of the community they represent. This is clearly an instance of the political alienation which is characteristic of classical parliamentary democracy, where public power is in the hands of the party leaders and not the people themselves.

The opposite case is one in which the delegates are completely limited by the mandate and are devoid of any right to negotiate and reach compromises. Then they either have to constantly communicate with someone who speaks in the name of the community and wait for authorization to make concessions, or adamantly refuse anything but the full satisfaction of the interests of their community. In the former case the community develops a bureaucracy *sui generis* which assumes the right to send instructions to the delegates according to its own will and outside of the democratic process. The latter alternative is a good example of communal particularism which blocks solution of any general problem or coerces the majority to make concessions. The consequence is considerable instability and inefficiency for the global society.

Both difficulties would be overcome in a system in which a principle of local autonomy would be reconciled with the principle of increasing freedom of the whole society without any mediating role of the political parties in the process of decision making. This means, first, that delegates of the community must be primarily responsible to their constituency and not to the political organization they are members of, and, second, that the delegates must be granted freedom to enter into dialogue with the delegates of other communities and together with them to look for solutions in the best long-range interests of both local communities and the whole federation. The delegates must be able to offer their constituencies a rational justification of these solutions and they have to be ready to resign if their justification is not accepted.

Such an idea of local autonomy involves an increase of equality at three different levels:

1. It is impossible for a community to lay down—by itself—its own laws, i.e., to be autonomous, unless class inequalities and inequalities in distribution of political power are removed. If local bosses, bureaucrats, and technocrats continue to monopolize economic and political power, local autonomy will only be a suitable ideological facade to conceal their actual domination and to protect it from the possible encroachment of higher authorities.

2. Local autonomy that is associated with active participation in determining basic policies for the whole society involves equality of rights of all communities. Under described conditions this formal equality, equality of right, grows into equality of condition.

3. Local autonomy conceived in an enlightened, rational way, with full consideration for the long-range interests of the whole society, becomes only a special case of universal human emancipation, which is at the same time the idea of growing equality of all individuals as human beings. The idea of emancipation means, on the one hand, abolition of all those repressive institutions and structures that thwart and deform human beings and, on the other hand, the creation of new forms of social organization that encourage personal development, favor imaginative and creative activity, and stimulate the growth of a wealth of needs of each individual.

There is no doubt that the general idea of freedom and of its special case, autonomy, can be interpreted in an entirely different way—as unrestricted production of both luxury and misery, meaningless waste and utter insecurity, spiritual isolation and degrading labor, superhuman power and frustrating impotency. This only shows that we should not support or resist pure ideas but rather the social forces that interpret them in one way or the other.

Patterns of Educational Change in the People's Republic of China

Long before the Communist revolution in China, a European sinologist remarked that the Chinese have been the most rebellious but the least revolutionary of peoples. The long history of China has recorded the rise and fall of a good number of dynasties, forming what has become known as the dynastic cycle. But cyclical motion implies repetition, and when a dynasty is replaced by another through rebellion, the national polity of China remains fundamentally unchanged. It is with this historical view in mind that the Communists have proclaimed themselves to be true revolutionaries. As revolutionaries, they have been motivated by an intense dissatisfaction with the old order and an equally intense desire to change that order. Both abandonment of the old and establishment of the new require all-out efforts at remaking the Chinese people, which is primarily an educational task.

How do the Communist revolutionaries view China's past in cultural and educational terms? Because of the centrality of Mao Tse-tung's role in the revolutionary movement, a quote from Mao will perhaps shed some light on this key question:

> There is in China an imperialist culture which is a reflection of the control of imperialism over China politically and economically. This form of culture is advocated not only by the cultural organizations run directly by the imperialists in China but also by a number of shameless Chinese. All culture that contains a slave ideology belongs to this category. There is also in China a semi-feudal culture which is a reflection of semi-feudal politics and economy and

99

has as its representatives all those who, while opposing the new culture and new ideologies, advocate the worship of Confucius, the study of the Confucian canon, the old ethical code and the old ideologies. Imperialist culture and semi-feudal culture are affectionate brothers, who have formed a reactionary cultural alliance to oppose China's new culture. This reactionary culture serves the imperialists and the feudal class, and must be swept away.

Within the semifeudal and semicolonial cultural context, education in "old" China, in the Communist view, merely served to perpetuate the rule of reaction and to impede China's progress toward modernity. Ideologically, education in the past is considered metaphysical and idealist in its philosophical orientation. Whether couched in the traditional philosophy of idealism to which the old feudal elements subscribed or in the vulgar evolutionism advocated by the modern bourgeoisie, the metaphysical approach to education stressed theory and book knowledge and was therefore totally divorced from practice.

In socioeconomic terms, "pre-liberation" education served the interests of the ruling classes to the exclusion of the exploited and oppressed masses. The time-honored tradition of dividing the society into the rulers and the ruled on the basis of education remained unchallenged in modern times. Despite isolated and individual efforts, education hardly reached the toiling masses, with the result that at the time of the Communist takeover illiteracy in China remained in the neighborhood of eighty percent of the population, giving rise to one of the most commonly used Communist slogans, that which proclaims China to be "poor and blank." Moreover, in the Communist view, the dismally few benefits education could bring to the Chinese economy went either for imperialist exploitation or for the consolidation of bureaucratic capitalism, resulting in the deepening of economic suffering on the part of the masses and the widening of social and cultural gulfs that separated the classes.

By renouncing and rejecting "old" education, the Communist leadership opened the way to introducing "new" education in a "new" China. This new education had to be developed for the creation of a new culture, a blueprint for which had been presented by Mao himself in his exceedingly important work "New Democracy," first published in 1940. The New Culture, according to Mao, must be "national, scientific and popular." When the Common Program was adopted in late 1949, following the founding of the People's Republic, these three guiding principles were incorporated into it and declared to be the objectives of the new state in the area of culture and education.

To be "national" is to develop a new set of educational ideas and practices that is in complete agreement with the objective conditions of China and is for the healthy growth of socialism based on Chinese creativity. National also implies the systematic elimination of all foreign influences that are detrimental to China's development as a sovereign, independent nation-state, although Mao did stress that "we should as far as possible draw on what is progressive in foreign culture for use in the development of China's new culture."

The "scientific" aspect involves two directly related objectives. The first has to do with the acceptance of the Communist definition of knowledge, which can be scientific only when it is dialectical and derived from practice. The importance of this doctrine can hardly be exaggerated because by so defining knowledge the Communists can bring about an educational revolution in the name of science and at the same time admit no contending schools of thought. Second, and in more concrete terms, for education to be scientific is to provide China with the urgently needed scientific and technical personnel on whom China's industrialization and economic development depend.

The doctrine of "popularism," or, as Mao put it, education for the masses, has grown out of the concept of class struggle. If education in old China failed to bring the benefits of education to members of the oppressed classes who formed the masses, education in the new China must reverse the situation and adopt a mass line. Again, in concrete terms, the Communists realize that the crucial goals of ideological indoctrination, economic development, social equalization, and cultural reorientation cannot be attained without the masses being educated to strive for them. It is in the spirit of popularism that many of the major innovations in education, ranging from literacy classes in the countryside in the early 1950s to the total suspension of the educational process in the cultural revolution of the mid-1960s, have taken place.

Up to the time of the Cultural Revolution, the development of education in China went through several notable stages. During the first, which lasted from 1949 to 1952, major efforts went into reorganization of the old and the creation of the new system. Foreign—predominantly American—supported schools on all levels were abolished and absorbed into the new national system, professional educators were subjected to varying degrees of thought reform, emphasis was placed on educating the masses, especially those in the rural areas, and new curriculum materials were produced for the new era in education. The second phase, from 1953 to 1957, corresponded with the first Five Year Plan and was generally considered the most impressive period of national reconstruction in spite of the many problems. This phase witnessed the steady expansion of educational facilities on all fronts, impressive gains in literacy, promotion of science and technology, and all-out emulation of the Soviet Union, which provided massive economic as well as educational assistance. With the advent of the Great Leap Forward movement in 1958, accompanied by the establishment of the communes, education expanded on all levels at a breakneck speed, under the reaffirmed principles of "education must be in the service of proletarian politics" and "education must be combined with productive labor." During this period, while statistical figures for both schools and students went up by leaps and bounds, overemphasis on politics and productive labor gave rise to very serious problems on all fronts, virtually disrupting the entire educational process which had been built up so painstakingly. It was to correct this tendency of stressing quantity at the expense of quality that the fourth phase of retrenchment was initiated in 1961. Although Redness and expertness remained as the major goals of education, there were clear signs that the latter should not be sacrificed for the former. Consequently, academic excellence was once again stressed and the amount of productive labor required of both educators and students was drastically reduced. It was also during this period of retrenchment that the principle of "two kinds of educational systems" was adopted and implemented. Sponsored by no less a personage than Liu Shao-ch'i, the new principle simply meant the maintenance of the status quo in regard to full-time schools, on the one hand, and all-out expansion of half-work, half-study schools, on the other. This policy was largely responsible for the stabilization of the educational scene up to the middle part of 1966. Then China was hit by the whirlwind of the Great Proletarian Cultural Revolution.

In both scope and intensity, the Cultural Revolution which began to rage out of control in the spring of 1966 undoubtedly represented the most sweeping and far-reaching phase of change in the entire history of China under Communism. It marked still another swing to the left of the pendulum of Chinese national life, largely as a result of the emergence of a new pattern during the period of retrenchment. To the zealous revolutionaries led by and identified with Mao himself, China in 1966 was showing every sign of abandoning the true objectives of revolution and compromising on the ideological front. Those in power, under the leadership of Liu Shao-ch'i, were accused of "taking the capitalist road" and of leading China down the path of "revisionism." The overriding purpose of the Cultural Revolution, therefore, was the seizure of power from the "revisionists" to create a new society in accordance with the blueprint of Mao.

To education, the Cultural Revolution meant not only the reversal of the revisionist trend but, more important, the mobilization of students as active agents of the revolution, which enabled them to wage revolutionary struggles on their own and to acquire the kind of experiences which would insure ideological correctness in the future. Known as the Red Guards, the student revolutionaries vigorously attacked what they contemptuously called "revisionist" education and demanded faithful adherence to the Maoist formula of socialist education.

In the context of the Cultural Revolution, the first significant statement by Mao concerning education was made on May 7, 1966, in a letter to Lin Piao, his newly designated heir-apparent, in which he directed that "the students' major concern is academic study, but they must study other subjects. This means they have to study not only liberal arts, but also engineering, agricultural and military sciences, as well as criticize the bourgeoisie. The curriculum must be shortened and there must be an educational revolution. The phenomenon in which our schools are dominated by bourgeois intellectuals cannot be allowed to continue." Inspired by what has since become known as the "May Directive" of Mao, several students at Peking University, led by a junior member of the faculty, on May 25, 1966, put up one of the first "big-character posters," which accused the president and other administrators of the university of following the capitalist principles and practices of education and thereby attempting to create a new generation of bourgeois intellectuals and to negate the achievements of socialist education. A few days later, Mao personally endorsed the revolutionary position of the students by ordering that the contents of the big-character poster be broadcast over Radio Peking. From then on, the educational part of the Great Cultural Revolution spread to all parts of the country, resulting in a complete reexamination of the educational record of China and the pouring forth of a variety of recommendations and demands for the restructuring of Chinese education.

It scarcely needs to be mentioned that the educational part of the Great Cultural Revolution was only one aspect of a much larger struggle, which coincided with the reassertion of power on the part of Mao and his supporters and the removal of Liu Shao-chi and those identified with his so-called revisionist policy lines from positions of power. In concrete terms, the educational revolution began with the dismissal of some of the top-ranking administrators in leading institutions, including such universities as Peking, Wuhan, Nanking, and many others. Without exception, these leading personalities were accused of reintroducing capitalism into Chinese education, going against the teachings of Chairman Mao, closing the doors of schools to members of the proletariat, encouraging intellectualism and with it social aloofness, and, in a word, following the road of revisionism. Once the responsible individuals were removed from positions of power, there followed a period in which the revolutionaries gave vent to their grievances and criticized all aspects of education at that time. Broadly, the Maoist revolutionaries were intensely dissatisfied with the fundamentally "traditional and capitalist" approach to education, which, in their view, manifested itself in several essential ways. First, the system by which educational opportunities were distributed was considered an unmistakable vestige of the discredited past in that the major means of selection continued to be competitive examination, reminiscent of the centuries-old imperial examination system. Continuation of this system meant, therefore, not only the rejection of promising students of proletarian origin who formed the majority, but also the creation of an academic minority or elite who were intellectually and psychologically opposed to the very essence of Maoist ideology. Second, emphasis upon academic performance, a natural byproduct of the examination system, had given rise to a situation in which the students were primarily concerned with academic excellence at the expense of politics. Third, the "revisionist" educational policy had defeated the very purposes of socialist education by weakening the students intellectually through "forced-feeding," morally through encouraging individualism, and physically through meaningless overwork.

The overthrow of "power-holders" was followed by a period of intense "power seizure" which was by no means confined to educational power. In the field of education, however, the downfall of what may be called the establishment, headed by Liu, led to a torrent of public criticism from all levels of education and all parts of the country. Whether general or specific, concerning theory or practice, all criticism had the common objective of Maoism. In the wake of such criticisms, a series of changes were introduced, some with the authority of the state and others by the new revolutionary committees which had taken over the administration of the majority of schools.

As far as the changes are concerned, abandonment of earlier beliefs and practices has been more prominent than adoption of new measures. As a direct response to the demands of revolutionary students, the Central Committee of the Chinese Communist Party and the State Council jointly announced the suspension of entrance examinations for all higher institutions on June 15, 1966. This act had the effect of releasing a considerable number of students for revolutionary activities, by and large through Red Guard organizations. The revolutionary activities of the Red Guards officially began on August 18, when Mao personally received the "revolutionary teachers and students" at Tien-an-men in Peking. From that day on, the students no longer concerned themselves with purely educational affairs but plunged into the all-encompassing task of "making revolution" on a nationwide basis.

In February and March, 1967, the Central Committee of the Chinese Communist Party issued, in quick succession, three directives ordering all students to return to their schools and to resume their revolutionary activities on campus. These directives exhorted the students to continue the Cultural Revolution in their own schools, to form alliances with the masses, to study Mao's works diligently, and, above all, to work out a plan for education in the future that would conform to the intent and spirit of the Cultural Revolution. Return to the schools, however, did not mean resumption of the educational process. Indeed, with the institutional framework irreparably smashed and the last vestige of former authority destroyed, it was physically impossible for a normal education process to go on. In the few schools where a semblance of normalcy prevailed, instruction was confined to the works of Mao.

Although primary and secondary schools began to resume their normal functions as early as 1968 under new revolutionary leadership and with drastically altered curricula, it was not until the summer of 1970 that institutions of higher learning started recruiting students. By the end of 1975, schools below the college level had fully recovered from the recent disruptions and enrollment was believed to be in the neighborhood of 135 million for elementary schools and 35 million for secondary schools. On the tertiary level, however, no more than 400,000 were in attendance, some twenty or so percent less than the pre–Cultural Revolution peak. Admission into higher institutions now follows four steps: individual application, mass recommendation, leadership review, and interview by the college or university concerned. Two or more years of working experience is imperative, but both age and academic limitations have been relaxed.

More than ten years after the outbreak of the Cultural Revolution, the education issue remains the center of political and ideological struggle in China today. Taking the past quarter of a century or more into consideration, one finds that, in spite of the zigs, zags, advances, and retreats on the educational front, there has been a dominant pattern of change in the steady deepening of Maoist thought on education that manifests itself in the tendency toward a more strict interpretation of Mao's ideas. Although in the earlier phase of its rule the Communist party struggled against the non-party and vestigial bourgeois elements, there is now a struggle within the party, between the so-called Maoist radicals on the one hand and the moderate pragmatists on the other.

It can be said without exaggeration that the kernel of Mao's thought or revolutionary philosophy is egalitarianism. With the means of production now firmly in the hands of the state, the only institution that is liable to give rise to both the idea and the reality of social elitism is education. Being thoroughly familiar with China's centuries-old tradition of rule by the educated elite, Mao believed that a revolution in education would go a long way in insuring the success of the larger socialist revolution, which has as its chief objective the elimination of social classes. In policy terms, Mao and his followers have advocated the "mass line," which stresses the overriding importance of proletarianizing the intellectuals and intellectualizing the proletariat.

In concrete terms, the Maoist mass line has called for the shortening of formal education because an unduly long duration of formal schooling is believed to lead to a state of mind in which the recipients of such education will develop attitudes of members of a special and privileged group, thus becoming aloof and divorced from the masses. It was this concern with the possible reemergence of an educated elite that prompted Mao to demand the shortening of the duration of primary education from six to five years, of secondary education from six to four or five years, and of higher education from five or four to two or three years. For the same reason, admission into higher institutions can come only after two or more years of productive labor, either on the farm or in the factory, for education without periodic exposure to the masses and actual working conditions is considered ideologically unsound and socially useless. Productive labor of all types has now become an integral part of the school programs on all levels. Urban schools either run their own factories or are linked up with neighboring factories where students perform a variety of work, while in rural areas educational programs in commune-run schools are invariably coordinated with the seasonal cycle of agricultural production.

The dispatch "up to the mountains and down to the fields" of some thirteen million young men and women after secondary schooling since the late 1960s has created problems of considerable complexity, but Mao insisted that the practice must go on in order to strengthen the young people's class consciousness and, with it, their revolutionary sense of dedication. Mao was strongly of the view that the inequality between urban and rural China can only be gradually removed through the steady development of the countryside by the efforts of the educated youth, while the disparity between those who use their brain and those who use their brawn can in time also be reduced and bridged.

The shortening of the years of formal schooling has been accompanied by a nationwide effort at simplifying the curriculum and teaching materials. For years, the peasants, workers, and members of the People's Liberation Army have been encouraged to take part in the decision-making process concerning not only the structure of education but also what is to be taught. For the formulation of curriculum and the writing and compilation of textbooks, reference works, teaching plans, and syllabi, the principles of applicability and comprehensibility have been stressed, on the ground that true knowledge comes only from practice. The role of teachers has, in pursuit of the mass line, undergone a major shift. Teachers are now expected to be responsive to the educational wishes and preferences of the masses, and academic achievements or professional expertness must be translated into constructive teaching instead of a sense of personal superiority. Furthermore, the authoritarian tradition which holds that a teacher can do no wrong has been subjected to severe criticism, and the teachers are asked to guide and help the students with a clear understanding of both their collective and individual needs.

Examination as a pedagogical device has been condemned, not so much for its being reminiscent of the centuries-old imperial examination system as its inherent emphasis upon competition, which inevitably leads to elitism of one form or another. Mao himself was convinced that the practice of admitting students through examination on the senior-middle-school and higher-education levels before the Cultural Revolution had been responsible for not only the rejection of promising students of proletarian origin who formed the majority, but also the creation of an academic elite who were intellectually and psychologically opposed to the very spirit of the mass line. To emphasize examination, therefore, is to encourage the students to seek academic excellence at the expense of proletarian politics, thereby defeating the purpose of socialist education.

Just as in sports and athletic events where the slogan "friendship first, competition second" is constantly repeated, in school work all students are encouraged to develop the spirit as well as the means of cooperation and to regard group progress as the true sign of educational achievement. Like the armed forces, which have abolished all ranks and insignia, institutions of education no longer award degrees or academic honors. Although professorial titles and salary differentials still exist, for more than ten years there have not been academic promotions, and those with relatively higher income most likely will be passed over when a nationwide increment in remuneration takes place. In short, to Mao and his faithful followers nothing is more important than the relentless search for equality in all aspects of Chinese national life, for which the Marxist theory and the revolutionary practice of class struggle provide the key.

In education, the changes introduced thus far all have the ultimate goal of removing inequality and insuring equality. While in the course of these changes new problems have appeared and have caused intraparty controversy and tension, the process of change has at the same time made clear certain trends that are significant for both the educational enterprise and Chinese society at large. There is, in the first place, the unmistakable trend toward what one may call the demystification of knowledge. Recalling the reverence accorded to mere literacy and even papers with written ideographs on them and the awe and esteem in which the literati were held, the popularization of education and, more important, the "dethroning" of the educated elite can only be regarded as a revolution with enormous psychological and intellectual implications. In this connection, even the economically disastrous Great Leap Forward experiment of the late 1950s was defended by Mao on educational grounds because the making of iron and steel by millions with the so-called backyard furnace had the effect of destroying the myth of modern science and of helping develop the "can-do" mentality among the masses.

The demystification process has been reinforced by the unrelenting propagation of the ideological theme of mass wisdom and creativity which is held to have been responsible for all the great cultural achievements of China in the past and will most certainly propel China to greater heights in the future. The current anti-Confucius campaign, aside from ideological considerations, clearly has the objective of doing away with the mystique and authority of the learned elite that had been composed of Confucian scholars for more than two thousand years. For the ideal of egalitarianism, Mao and his followers seem determined to eliminate the top rung of China's social pyramid by exhorting the masses to fight against any form of professionalism, bureaucratism, meritocracy, or technocracy. Expertness means only greater capacity to serve the people; expertness without Redness or the proper political consciousness can only lead to social inequality.

Of equal significance has been the process of decentralization of the educational enterprise. Since the very concept of professional expertise has been rejected, the important task of creating a new educational system throughout China has been entrusted to the masses, who form the "three-in-one unity" represented by the peasants, the workers, and the soldiers in one combination and by the party, the teachers, and the students in another. Local initiative and self-reliance are encouraged with a view to coordinating educational work with the productive, social, and cultural needs of the local community. Peasants, workers, and members of the armed services have been brought into the schools for both instructional and administrative purposes, to insure against usurpation of educational leadership by politically less reliable elements.

In any event, the educational experiment in China, especially since the Cultural Revolution of the mid-1960s, represents the most ambitious attempt at human engineering ever undertaken, seeking, as one observer of the scene remarked, to "heighten man's awareness of the objective laws of motion in human society and nature and his subjective capacity to change reality within these laws." China under the Maoists has rejected both the traditional Chinese and the modern Western models; what comes out of the new experiment in education will no doubt have a profound impact on the shape of China in the future.

Bibliography

Barendson, Robert D. *Half-Work, Half-Study Schools in Communist China: Recent Experiments in Self-supporting Educational Institutions.* Washington, D.C.: United States Office of Education, 1964.

Chen, Theodore H. E., *Thought Reform of the Chinese Intellectuals.* Hong Kong: University of Hong Kong Press, 1960.

Cheng, C. Y. *Scientific and Engineering Manpower in Communist China.* Washington, D.C.: National Science Foundation, 1965.

Gardner, John, and Wilt, Idema. "China's Educational Revolution." In *Authority Participation and Cultural Change in China,* edited by Stuart Schramm. Cambridge: Cambridge University Press, 1973.

Hu C.-T. *Chinese Education under Communism.* Rev. ed. New York: Teachers College Press, 1974.

Lewis, John W., ed. *Party Leadership and Revolutionary Power in China.* Cambridge: Cambridge University Press, 1970.

Munro, Donald J. "Egalitarian Ideal and Educational Fact in Communist China." In *China: Management of a Revolutionary Society,* edited by John M. H. Lindbeck. Seattle: University of Washington Press, 1971.

Price, Ronald T. *Education in Communist China.* London: Routledge and Kegan Paul, 1970.

Ridley, C. P. et al. *The Making of a Model Citizen in Communist China.* Stanford, Calif.: Hoover Institution, 1971.

Schurmann, Franz. *Ideology and Organization in Communist China.* Berkeley: University of California Press, 1966.

RONALD R. EDMONDS

Alternative Patterns for the Distribution of Social Services

Institutions of social service are nonprofit agencies whose purposes are to assist groups and individuals to maintain or advance themselves in the social order. Schools, adoption agencies, welfare agencies, and counseling centers are all examples of social service settings.

We now know that as a social order we are least effective in delivering social service to those who are impoverished, of color, physically handicapped, or otherwise different in ways that are observable. The literature that describes the social pathology of our response to such individuals is both substantial and persuasive. Perusing that literature from the perspective of my own experiences as teacher, researcher, and administrator persuades me that our "bad" social service institutions are, for the most part, staffed by "good" men and women. Certainly there are teachers, social workers, doctors, and administrators who are racist, autocratic, ethnocentric, and, in general, personally and professionally repulsive. I do not believe such individuals constitute the norm among social servants. I rather believe that most social servants are decent men and women who work hard and conscientiously strive to benefit the needful portions of our population. If you are prepared to accept such a characterization of social service settings and the people who staff them, you must acknowledge the paradox of bad social service being delivered by good people.

This discussion is principally directed to those of good intention and thwarted purpose who daily participate in the paradox that is the object of these remarks. The paradox need not continue; my own experience illustrates that social service settings, which serve all manner of American minorities, can be effective, efficient, and, most important, respectful of those to be served.

I make this last point because being respectful of those to be served is the minimal prerequisite to effective social service. A technically competent teacher who is disrespectful of students and parents cannot create or maintain that mood of consensus and co-operation that characterizes a good school. Effective social service reform must be characterized by both technical proficiency and an institutional climate that acknowledges and respects the unique characteristics of the client population.

My design for betterment has three parts which, taken together, describe a method of successful intervention in social service delivery. First, clients must become as influential as constituents in defining the uses to which the social service setting will be put; second, the social servants, as internal advocates for reform, must develop and articulate a "maximal" concept of effective social service; third, the community to which the service is to be delivered must adopt the "utility of minimums" as the conceptual basis for describing improved social service.

Clients are those individuals with whom the institution has direct contact, those who are present to receive the social service. Constituents are those on whose behalf the social service is made available. When a teacher is teaching, the students are clients. When an adoption worker arranges permanent parentage, the child being placed is a client.

Identifying constituents is more difficult, but may be made easier by putting the question, to whom do the teacher and other social servants think they must answer for their professional conduct? The teacher's answer may describe a group as small as an elected board of education or as large as the entire population of the school district. The group to whom the teacher feels accountable is a constituency. Of particular importance in this discussion is the frequency with which social servants answer this hypothetical query by describing a population that does not include their clients.

Constituency is a dynamic concept and may vary from social

servant to social servant. At the core of the concept of constituency is the notion of representing interests and standards. The social servant who seeks internal reform must come to understand that the aura of respect I mentioned earlier requires perceiving clients as synonymous with constituents when interests and standards are being articulated.

Effective social service settings need not perceive all constituents as clients, but all clients must be perceived as constituents. It is a general principle of good social service that the constituent population is larger than the client population. Thus any institution that serves large numbers but is answerable to small numbers cannot effect good social service.

By its very nature, social service requires a norm. Whether the social servant is a teacher, social worker, or counselor, there must be a standard of personal attainment toward which the client is to move. In the instance of schooling, the norm may be as tangible as minimal competence in reading, writing, and computing or as intangible as the teacher's perception of pupil behaviors that demonstrate socialization. "Good" school districts confer school skills that are explicitly or implicitly a response to parental consensus on the school skills prerequisite to mastery of the successive levels of schooling. Such socialization as may occur in a good school derives its description of socialized behaviors from educator perception of parental behavior norms. School districts that are "bad" or that become "bad" do so largely because of failure to effect or maintain a community dynamic characterized by responsiveness to the community such as I have described for "good" school districts.

In adoption, the norm may be placing a child in a family. In counseling, the norm may be full, useful, and gainful employment. These personal attainments are the objects of social service and the end toward which the social servant strives as he works with clients.

A basic issue in social service reform is the origin of the norm of personal attainment that describes successful social service. It is a premise of this discussion that successful social service can never be managed in a setting in which the norms are developed in consultation with constituents but not with clients. In the instance of primary schooling, for example, the teacher can never be instructionally successful when the standards of pupil performance are derived from groups that do not include a preponderance of the parents of the pupils.

Adoption agencies whose placement practices are designed to serve the parenting needs of adults with only modest attention to the parental needs of children cannot manage effective placement for all children who are adoptable. In the same way, counselors who define useful and gainful employment in exclusive consultation with employers can never offer employment counseling that will be in the best interests of clients. In each instance, the social service's disability has its origin in the social servant's perception of a constituency that need not include clients.

The social servants who do not perceive of clients as constituents usually develop a set of professional behaviors that are proprietary and culturally autocratic. One of the clichés in social service rhetoric is that "we must help our clients to help themselves." That is a good cliché and forms a simple and proper basis for evaluating the appropriateness of the social servant's professional behavior. Clients in social service are being helped most when they are provided the means to greater appreciation and utilization of their own skills and resources. Recognizing client skills and resources that can be cultivated requires respectful appreciation of the unique characteristics that describe all individuals. Interacting with individuals on the basis of definition and standards that are not developed in close consultation with those individuals precludes insight into the skills and resources that they may possess.

First, the definitions often turn out to be inaccurate. That there are impoverished Americans of color who are culturally deprived, cognitively deficient, and otherwise pathological is certainly true. That the incidence of such individual disability is as great as social service institutions would like to believe is certainly not true. Social service programs predicated on such a profound misrepresentation are bound to be ineffective.

The second mischievous consequence of the imposition of a definition of client need is the effect on the social service milieu. When institutions compel individuals to conform to a set of capricious and autocratic expectations, abrasive interaction invariably occurs. If the social servant does not question the imposing of definitions of client need, then the social servant behaves as a stereotypical, rigid bureaucrat, with a manner that is offensively arrogant. If the social servant has misgivings about the autocracy of his institution, then his behavior is either defensive or ambiguous and otherwise not helpful to the social service needs of the client.

Improving the quality of interaction in social service settings that impose definitions of need is a virtually impossible task. Neither staff courses in group dynamics nor sensitivity sessions can alter the fundamental inappropriateness of institutional practice that is not mindful of the unique character of those to be served.

Defining clients as constituents creates a process of institutional decision making that can avoid or overcome these dangers. In the instance of schooling, educator consultation with parents, when such consultation is instrumental in defining instructional purposes, may profoundly alter the standard to be used in measuring satisfactory pupil progress. Since standards of pupil progress must, for the foreseeable future, remain normative, it is essential that the parents of pupils be instrumental in the establishment of the norm if schools wish to work in a milieu characterized by community acceptance of, and support for, the instructional goals of the school. The most singly pervasive characteristic of successful schooling is consensus within and between school and community on the uses to which the school is to be put. Parent accusations of teacher arrogance, indifference, or antipathy can be avoided only when parents can observe the positive relationship between their interests and the school's behavior.

Institutional response to parental interests cannot occur unless one of two circumstances prevail. The school can be in cultural conformity to the community of which it is a part. This often occurs in middle-class suburbs or rural settings characterized by minimally satisfactory income and cultural homogeneity. In circumstances of cultural homogeneity and consensus, the school's policies and procedures are rarely distant from the interests and expectations of the community. Teachers are so like the families they serve, and so attuned to the social dynamic and community milieu that describes the community, that they invariably reflect the interests and disposition of the families of the children they serve.

In instances in which the community to be served is ethnically, racially, culturally, or economically different from the middle-class milieu that characterizes teachers and schools, teachers cannot rely on their intuitive understanding of the community to know how best to proceed when the purpose is pupil progress that is both acceptable to, and appreciated by, the community. Such a circumstance requires school personnel to make parents and community representatives explicitly instrumental in determining the programs and instructional activities of the school. The community must be chiefly responsible for the school's perception of which bodies of knowledge and sets of skills will best prepare students to be of service to the community.

Thus clients become synonymous with constituents when, and only when, the social servant's definition of community need is principally determined by information provided by those to be served. Teachers thus develop standards of pupil performance principally as a function of interaction with the parents of their pupils. When this happens, the probability of misdiagnosis of instructional need is dramatically reduced. Of equal importance, parents can observe the consequences of their willingness to share with instructional personnel parental standards for instruction and parental definition of the schooling needs of their children.

I turn now to the second part of my design. In recent years, great efforts have been made at institutional reform. Substantial numbers of social servants have pursued a variety of strategies intended to alter the basis on which their institutions operated. These efforts have produced only modest gains in relation to need and effort. These tactical failings have most often occurred because of a failure to identify those fundamental institutional characteristics from which the disability flows. The most effective internal advocacy of reform depends on the advocate's addressing himself to the basic premises that describe the institution.

Social service practice is dictated by administrative rules and regulations. Institutional rules and regulations proceed from policy.

Policy proceeds from premises which are a function of the policy maker's values and attitudes. This reform effort within an institution should be directed to those decisions that are of the most importance because their consequences are pervasive. Reform efforts that are exclusively invested in administration or policy rarely yield the gains that are sought.

Adoption agencies are a case in point. Substantial numbers of social workers in adoption agencies have struggled to alter the nature of service in their agencies. These internally generated reforms have usually consisted of activities such as recruitment of minority professional personnel, increased community contact in the form of addresses to civic groups and media descriptions of the agencies' services, and an effort to streamline the processing of prospective parents. These activities are usually intended to increase the number of children placed, especially those defined as "hard to place." The "hard to place" are children of color, children with physical or mental handicaps, or children over six months of age. The kinds of activities described rarely generate levels of gain that satisfy the expectations of the internal reform advocates. More important, the gains do not bring the agency to levels of service that meet the needs of children who are not being served. This discussion proceeds on the assumption that no child in the custody of an adoption agency should wait more than six months for permanent placement.

The tactical failure of many internal reform efforts is a function of their superficial relationship to the origin of the institution's behavior. Both administrative practice and policy proceed from the institution's basic notions of the uses to which the setting should be put. Thus one can manage considerable change in administrative practice only to discover that new policies and their subsequent administration recreate the negative circumstances that initially prompted the effort at internal reform.

The social servant is in a unique position to discern the fundamental premises to which I refer. Participation in the internal life of an institution offers one the opportunity to observe that staff respond to behavioral parameters set forth in institutional policy. Access to policy makers in a context of shared understanding of the institution and shared information that precisely describes institutional behavior lends itself to pursuit of the question, What is the origin of the policy makers' disposition to implement certain goals and standards of institutional behavior?

In the instance of adoption, for example, recruitment of minority staff is a modest reform because staff of an institution usually behave in conformity to institutional policy. If policy is defective, the mere presence of minority staff will not improve administrative behavior. Minority staff may be sought to encourage applications from prospective minority parents, to make processing more comfortable, etc. If the criterion for successful service is the placement of more "hard-to-place" children, minority staff may discover that they are participating in a process that neither increases minority applications nor makes parent processing more comfortable. Thus, despite the presence of minority staff, placement for children of color may not improve.

This discussion proceeds on the assumption that most adoption agencies have premises that are profoundly unresponsive to children. We come, then, to the basic perspective that describes the institutional approach to adoption and the impact of that premise on serving children. In the United States, the function of adoption is to serve adults who wish to have children. Adoption agencies define their purpose as "creating families," "placing children in appropriate homes," etc. Such language should be considered in the context of the overall approach to placement that describes adoption agencies. In general, adults are being evaluated to discover whether or not they are deserving of the service the agency has to offer. Hence, rigorous and extensive tests must be passed if one is to qualify as a parent. The emphasis in the whole of this is on adults, not children.

Most adoption agencies prefer prospective parents who are biologically incapable of parentage. That is so because American adoption came into being as a consequence of the same ideology that produced compensatory education. The American norm is observable virility in men and maternity in women. The observable proof of one's passing the test of manliness and womanliness, thus defined, is biological offspring. Failure to produce offspring deprives society of its superficial test of sexual acceptability and con-

119

formity. Individuals who cannot pass the test thus seek the means to mask their failure. It is in this context that one should consider adoption workers' preoccupation with physical matching. Further, the purpose of the historic secrecy surrounding adoption was not to benefit the child but to assist the adoptive parents in their masquerade as virile man and fertile woman.

The preceding is descriptive of certain early premises that characterized adoption. The rhetoric of adoption has evolved sufficiently to emphasize children, but that rhetoric does not proceed from a decision to make adoption a child-centered service. Thus adoption policies and practices continue to flow from an adult-oriented premise of service while social servants struggle to develop practices that will better serve children. One should consider the language that is used to describe any agency that lacks children for placement. Great lamentation is raised because needful adults are being deprived of the trappings of manliness and womanliness. An agency defining itself as child-centered would rejoice that there seemed to be fewer needful children than at an earlier moment.

One further point should be made in this regard. When agencies say they lack children, they usually mean they lack normal, white infants. Consider the ideology of service and cultural perspective that allows a social service agency to say it has insufficient children for placement while retaining custody of great numbers of children who are of color, over six months old, or physically or emotionally handicapped. The agency's dismissal of such children as "hard to place" or "unadoptable" is illustrative of cultural autocracy in two ways. First, there is the bias against peoples of color which makes serving children of color less urgent than serving children who are white. Second, placement of children who are different in the ways described does not facilitate masking the infertile adult by placing a child who is "matched" so as to seem a biological offspring of the infertile adult. Each of these culturally autocratic illustrations proceeds from an ethnocentric perception of constituency. That social servants define their constituents as white, even when serving clients of color, is fairly easy to discern. In the same sense, the effort to aid the infertile in seeming fertile proceeds from perceiving of constituents as normal by virtue of their biological parentage while the clients are deficient by virtue of their infertility.

Observation of these and other behaviors of any institution ought to raise serious questions about the uses to which the setting is being put. More important, internal reformers should proceed from the general principle that effective reform depends on access to those who define the uses to which a setting is being put. Given limited energies and resources, reform effort should bypass ascending levels of administration and decision making in pursuit of those individuals or that group from whom the institutional definition flows.

Every institutional behavior that has its origin in the culturally autocratic premises described earlier must be eliminated. Moreover, the adoption agency must so define itself as to preclude further policies and practices that proceed from cultural autocracy. This requires analysis that goes beyond particular policy practice to a basic premise such as the adoption agency's perception of constituency.

The language of internal change should be grand. My intent in making this suggestion is that the social servant engage in an analysis of his role as a social servant that will bring him to a subservient and receptive frame of mind. The proper interaction between a social servant and the community he serves is one in which the social servant strives to understand how his professional resources can best advance the interests and needs of those he serves. The scenario I seek in my reference to "grand" is as follows.

The social servant begins by committing himself to the most auspicious standard of service. For example, the teacher vows "to prepare each student for the fullest realization of his intellectual and academic potential and the most positive participation in his community." Implementing such a standard necessitates criteria for judging academic and intellectual progress. Thoughtful social servants will soon recognize that "academic and intellectual potential" has no meaning outside of a community context. Realizing potential requires having some sense of the range of community need that should be addressed. It may well be that urban, black communities have greater need for architects than veterinarians. What this is

121

intended to suggest is that parental and community perception of pupil progress is bound to be more tangible than the abstract goals to which schools commit themselves.

In such a context of analysis, the social servant is brought to the question, what does the community need? Answering such a question identifies the social frame within which academic and intellectual progress can be assessed. When the community in question is of color, or otherwise different from the cultural context that describes a school, it becomes necessary to develop intimate insight into the community to answer the question of community need. Once community enters into the social servant's implementation of the auspicious standard to which he has committed himself, representatives of the community begin to be perceived as the sources of intimate insight needed to ascertain community need.

The particular bodies of knowledge and sets of skills to be conveyed to the students derive from intimate interaction between the teacher, the parents, and other representatives of the community. The social servant's own analysis has thus moved from the grandiose and the abstract to the tangible and the practical. Equally important, the social servant has come to understand that the best social service requires definition by those to be served. Once the teacher is brought to the realization that he cannot do his job to his own satisfaction without the help and guidance of those he is to serve, there comes into being the accepting frame of mind that can make clients become constituents.

The substance of this process should be interest in a more culturally neutral setting. Blaming the victim and requiring individuals to meet institutional expectations are manifestations of cultural autocracy. The process of utilizing a description of the maximum social service outcome of institutional behavior eventually brings one to the substantive concept of cultural democracy as the basic premise from which an institution proceeds. The parent-teacher consultation described above is culturally democratic. Cultural democracy is a circumstance in which difference is acknowledged, understood, and appreciated.

The preceding is directed to internal institutional change. I turn now to externally imposed institutional change, which is the third part of my design. The nature of external intervention in the life of an institution imposes dramatically different perspectives on how best to make progress. The recommendations made earlier regarding tactical perspectives on internal change have disastrous consequences when used by community advocates.

However, community demands are often couched in the language of maximums. Black students often demand "education that is responsive to black needs." Black parents often demand "education that will help our children realize their potential." Such language is tactically disastrous when the goal is institutional improvement. Abstract and grandiloquent description of the desirable outcomes of institutional behavior deprives the intervener of unambiguous measures for assessing institutional behavior.

What is wanted is a concept of institution-intervener interaction that will describe proper behavior for both. It is the responsibility of the institution to pursue lofty goals and to take fullest advantage of the bodies of knowledge and sets of skills the staff represent. It is the responsibility of the community to know precisely what service it seeks and to have criteria for determining whether or not that service is being made available.

For example, schools describe themselves as teaching citizenship, civility, respect for others, and equally insubstantial characteristics. The words describe the maximum of institutional attainment. By their very nature, such goals preclude external observation and evaluation. Institutional decision makers in a community exchange based on such language are protected from accountability, partly because the nature of the dialogue does not require the decision makers to precisely articulate the service that is being delivered. Who knows whether or not citizenship is being taught? Parental interest in other services, such as reading, can be shunted aside by being placed in the larger context of the institution's presumed teaching of citizenship and equally abstract skills.

Allowing an institution to publicly commit itself only to grand and abstract goals leaves the institution free to use its own judgment of how best to pursue its goals and to describe whether or not progress is being made almost entirely on the basis of the social servants' feelings about what is going on. I use the word *feelings* to emphasize the imprecise and subjective language that must be used in discussing the abstract language of maximum institutional outcome.

The above may seem to contradict my earlier suggestion that the internal change agent should be grand in articulating his concept of social service. The purpose of the internal change agent's exercise is to identify the origin and nature of the uses to which the setting should be put. Having done that, clients should be instrumental in determining the appropriateness of the definition. Using grand language in community-institution dialogue is inappropriate unless all parties in the dialogue agree that acceptable levels of service are being attained. Such is rarely the case. Institution-community dialogue usually occasions community effort to improve service. Thus those who staff the social service setting should enter the dialogue in a subservient frame of mind, prepared to respond to the description that is put forward by community spokesmen.

Now consider the tactical efficacy of community use of the language of minimums in discussing whether or not a social service institution is fulfilling its obligation to serve community needs. The community advocate faces four distinct tactical necessities. First, he must generate constituency or coalition to be able to profit from describing himself as representing substantial numbers, or the interests of substantial numbers. Second, he must effectively manage the public process of making demands of the institutional decision makers. Third, he must have criteria for evaluating institutional response to his demands, which criteria must meet the test of being acceptable to his constituency or coalition. Fourth, he must be prepared to articulate the actions to be taken by the community, depending on the outcome of the demands that are made of the institution. Each of these processes recommends the utility of minimums as the most effective tactical instrument.

Ordinarily, constituency or coalition grows out of community response to a visible spokesman who uses language that is dramatic, general, and vaguely responsive to such disquiet as may exist in the community in response to inadequate social service. Coalescing around vague demands such as "the schools should communicate with parents better" or "kids should get more out of being in school"

124

is a very superficial and potentially disabling basis on which to generate constituency or coalition. The parties to this process have little sense of whether, and at what level, their interests coincide. Such groups often flounder when compelled to deal with specific institutional response to vague community demands.

This discussion suggests that it is better to postpone community coalition than establish it on the basis of abstract maximums that will not survive confrontation. Community dialogue that seeks minimum and precise description of acceptable institutional behavior constitutes a firm basis on which to found constituency and coalition. For example, few parents would resist reading, writing, and computation as a minimal description of proper educational outcome. The sophisticated community advocate will discern the radical implications of community consensus on the desirability of universal primary pupil acquisition of these basic school skills. In fact, schools, as presently constituted, cannot effect universal primary pupil acquisition of these basic school skills.

There will be many in the group who will articulate interest in discipline, human relations, group dynamics, and a variety of other interesting, but imprecise, educational outcomes. Such goals should be resisted on the grounds that schools might well accept any or all of them without incurring the obligation to deliver observable and evaluable institutional behavior.

If the community advocate has been persuasive in his advocacy of universal primary pupil acquisition of basic school skills as the definition of the community's standard of schooling, then the stage is set for making good use of the confrontation that should occur. The central substantive issue is the community's response to "universally" successful primary pupil mastery of schooling. That means that no child free of certifiable handicap will be expected to acquire less than the community's definition of basic school skills.

Educator rejection of such a notion proceeds from two culturally autocratic premises. First, there is the widespread educator belief that pupil home life and social milieu are the principal causes of pupil performance. Second, there is the educator rejection of community definition of schooling when the community does not fulfill the educator's cultural expectations of what a community should be.

Both premises have the effect of placing the burden of performance on pupils with no concomitant responsibility for teachers. It is in such a context that educators reject universally successful primary pupil mastery of basic school skills as a standard. Assuming that parents have a more accurate perception of their children's abilities than such educators, there will be dramatic educator-community disagreement on the utility of universal primary pupil acquisition of basic school skills.

The community advocate can, therefore, predict dramatic confrontation based on either the school's refusal to accept such a goal or its inability to meet it. As a result, as time goes on the coalition or constituency will grow more cohesive, partly because of the precision of their shared interests and partly because of their shared rejection of the institution's inability or refusal to meet so reasonable and seemingly modest a demand as universal primary pupil acquisition of basic school skills. If such demands can be extracted from community and coalition dialogue, the opportunity for a deceptively dramatic presentation to institutional decision makers then presents itself. Extensive public notice should be taken of the presentation, more because of the advocate's representation of substantial numbers than because of the initial drama of the substance of the demands that are being made.

The tactical value of external institutional intervention, predicated on the tangible nature of the language of minimums, allows a calendar of response to be made a part of the presentation. The schools might be given an academic year in which to demonstrate substantial progress toward the goals. In Michigan, each community is annually provided with a public description of pupil performance. Such public information lends itself to the process that is being suggested. Any community that can agree on what constitutes minimally successful schooling has accomplished the first major step toward annual description of the primary school's competence.

The nature of the community demand being made logically proceeds to subsequent objective evaluation of the nature of movement toward the goal. Evaluation of minimal and precise institutional outcomes predicts two possibilities. There may be school

126

systems that do, in fact, manage universal primary pupil acquisition of basic school skills. Such an event could occur only as a consequence of radical alteration in institutional behavior. There is not now, nor has there ever been in the United States, a school district that has managed to teach all primary pupils free of certifiable handicap to read, write, and compute to demonstrable levels of minimal competence. Therefore, any societal circumstances causing such a school district to come into being would be a success of the first order.

It is more likely that the school district will not have attained universal pupil acquisition of basic school skills, and that failure will have occurred substantially along class lines. Such a moment confronts a community with the flagrantly discriminatory concept of social service that describes its schools and other public institutions. The confrontation cannot occur in the absence of unambiguous evaluation of institutional response to reasonable community expectations. The predictable school response to such a confrontation will consist of blaming the victim. The struggle is thus defined between the community advocate and his institutional protagonist. At issue will be a basic question such as can schools be held responsible for children who violate institutional expectations by reason of culture, class, or color?

The community advocate, in articulating minimal performance standards to be applied to the institution, has engaged in a reform effort with auspicious cultural and political implications. Culturally, the language of minimums seeks to neutralize a hostile social service setting. The neutrality occurs because the institution is being made to do the community's bidding.

Three important factors relating to this discussion should be emphasized. First, the community advocate now represents the community with a set of specific and measurable institutional goals. Second, all resources for change can gravitate toward the precise and minimal reform agenda that has been articulated. Third, and most important, the tactics under discussion offer the greatest possibility of success in making social service institutions more responsive to poor and minority communities. What is wanted is eventual success that will persuade poorly served communities that they need not despair of improvement in the quality of social service now available to them. What is being tactically recommended is that such communities initially concentrate their reform energies on precise agreement and definition of minimally acceptable schooling and other social services.

In sum, my purpose has been to articulate a set of behaviors which might profitably engage the energies of a substantial number of men and women who are dissatisfied with the quality of social service. The process I have proposed combines elements of participatory decision making, community control, and organized community action. The substance of my suggestions is that cultural and institutional autocracy be replaced by an appreciation for difference that is best summarized as cultural democracy. Thus might our social service settings become instruments of equity for us all.

WAYNE A. O'NEIL

An Alternative for U.S. Education: Teaching Minority People to Study Their Own Cultures

I begin by commenting at some length on the problems endemic to American education, to an educational system in a capitalist society. I then move on to sketch what the character of education would likely be in a left-libertarian industrial society, in a socialist society. I close by filling out part of that sketch to somewhat modest proportions. I see no particular reason to believe that there will be any significant change in the situation that I characterize briefly here in the beginning of this essay, thus no reason to expect that the utopia I then sketch in will exist anywhere—least of all in America—in the near future. Capitalism is not in a state of imminent collapse, nor in its dying stages—despite what some on the left may say or write. Still, it is best to be prepared for that collapse or for the pulling down of it from within or without, good to have thought things through just in case and to know how to conduct oneself in the meantime. Kropotkin, in beginning to answer the question posed in the title of his long essay "Must We Occupy Ourselves with an Examination of the Ideal of a Future System?," wrote:

I believe that we must.

In the first place, in the ideal we can express our hopes, aspirations and goals, regardless of practical limitations, regardless of the degree of realization which we attain; for this degree of realization is determined purely by external causes.

In the second place, the ideal can make clear how much we are infected with old prejudices and inclinations. If some aspects of

129

everyday life seem to us so sacred that we dare not touch them even in an analysis of the ideal, then how great will our daring be in the actual abolishment of these everyday features? In other words, although daring in thought is not at all a guarantee of daring in practice, mental timidity in constructing an ideal is certainly a criterion of mental timidity in practice.[1]

I agree. And with this kind of preparation we can be ready—come the revolution—to replace the institutions of capitalism with institutions of our own making.

There is a further point to this enterprise of constructing alternatives in our heads now. At the present time, at the edges of the empire I believe it is possible, just possible, that a partial reorganization of American institutions, education among them, can take place. Such things can happen there—in American Indian communities, say, or in black communities in the rural South—because these despised and isolated minorities are of little or no consequence to the proper working of the American economic machine. Thus the reorganization of education that I describe below has relevance —perhaps—to only these people in the present historical context. I do not mean to limit my utopia to America's outcasts; it's just that anyone that really matters to the proper working of the system —whether that person be in the active or reserve labor force—is to that extent not free to operate outside the institutions of the system, not free to reorganize them or control them. But people at the margins of the system are free to reorganize marginal institutions, education among them.

Indeed, except among the outcasts, we are at present witnessing, following a brief period of laissez-faire in matters educational, a re-rationalization of the educational system. Experiments aimed at reducing its dullness and restrictiveness are now understood to have been counterproductive, and the necessity (brought on by the condition of the job market, not by any upgrading of necessary job skills) for more and more people to go on into higher education is leading to the destruction of the spirit of free inquiry that has hitherto been available in even the most benighted of our colleges and universities. The present debate over declining scores and skills, the raising high of traditional standards, the march back to grades and to basics, the redistribution of the educational wealth from higher education into essentially vocational educational institutions masking as colleges: these things are all part of the rationalization of a system that had gotten slightly—but only slightly—out of hand.[2]

Thus a certain limited amount of control that some Americans have been able to exercise over their lives, in the schools, in neighborhood action groups (on rent control for example), and in other areas of life, is now being denied. There are not only economic gains to be lost in the present state of the economy: the present state of the polity is forcing social and political losses as well.

What's Wrong with American Education?

In a word it is capitalism that is wrong with it, plain and simple. Real education is almost incidental for the most part for most people in most schools: they are provided with relatively limited computational skills and the reading and writing skills necessary to participate as obedient and reliable workers and consumers in the political economy. That is the end of education for the overwhelming majority of Americans. Beyond offering this rudimentary education, schools exist primarily to inculcate the virtues required of an obedient public and to regulate the flow of job seekers into the labor market.

The attitudes toward work and consumption inculcated in the course of school education are the obvious ones: docility, respect for authority—or at least the fear of challenging it—promptness, the disconnectedness of things and phenomena. It is in the schools that the alienation of thought from action is first effected. The notion that work is work and that pleasure is pleasure, that never the twain do meet, is emphasized in the very routine of school and recess and vacation and athletics. Young people march out of the schoolhouse convinced that for the most part things as they are are the way "they 'spozed to be."

Schools are also used to regulate the flow of young people into the labor market, generally now—given the progressive automation and/or overseas flight of American industry—to delay and restrict that flow. It is in this context that we should understand the vet-

131

erans' educational subsidy that has been in effect almost without break since the end of World War II—the war that solved the disastrous unemployment problem that characterized the general economic collapse we now refer to, almost with fondness, as the Great Depression. We should view the laws written late in the Depression that restricted the participation of America's youth in the labor force in a similar way,[3] as we should such proposals as the recent one of the Secretary of Education of the Commonwealth of Massachusetts that the availability of public education be extended to fourteen years to help solve the unemployment problem in the state.

Thus as there is less and less need for the number of workers that become available to enter the labor force, the amount of education (in terms of the number of school years completed, not in terms of things known—the latter remains more or less fixed) demanded by an employer increases, with various certificates and diplomas becoming required for jobs whose essentially semi-skilled nature has not changed. The school-leaving age is in this way increased by both law and hiring practices.

Under these conditions there is no content added to education to fill out the increased number of school years required, for none is needed. What used to occupy, say, eight years of school must now be stretched out to fill fourteen years—with the same empty job still waiting outside beyond the schoolhouse door. The door is a different one, the door of a junior or community college, the certificate is a bit fancier, but nothing else has changed in any very noticeable way. Schools have become giant detention centers, more like prisons or army training camps than they are like the campuses of the schools, colleges, and universities of the ruling class.

In this light it is interesting to examine the attempts of bourgeois social scientists and their spokesmen in the popular media to explain the decline in reading, writing, and computational skills and the decade-long decline in ACT and SAT scores.[4] They are of course unwilling or incapable of looking very far for answers, although they are quick enough to propose solutions to the problems as they see them: get back to the old days and the old ways of educating people. A leading candidate for the best non-explanation

132

of the year (academic year) was recently reported widely in the popular media: the SAT scores, etc., have fallen off because the people taking the tests now are the younger brothers and sisters (more sisters than brothers) of those giants who clipped off the higher scores of yesteryear.[5] Now here is why younger siblings perform worse than older ones: it is because they are raised in a more intellectually (IQ) impoverished environment than the older ones. This fact can be demonstrated in the following way: say that parents with IQ's of 100 and 110 have a child. Of course at birth the child has no measurable IQ, but it can be assumed to be 0. Thus the average IQ of the three people who make up this nuclear family is 70; that is the IQ of the child's environment. Two years later a second child is born and since the older child has still no IQ to show for its two years on this earth, the average now falls to 52.5. Things get worse the faster the children come into the world, the more the children are left with just one of the parents, with a baby-sitter of an inconsequential IQ, or to themselves. In any case the older child has more of what there is to get simply by virtue of having arrived on the scene sooner.* The lessons for family planning are obvious. Falstaff in gathering together a company of foot soldiers with which to serve Prince Hal is driven to recruiting the "younger sons of younger brothers"; now they are left to the junior colleges.

Explanations of similar depth—statistically neat and intellectually vacuous—abound, but it does not seem to me that adequate explanations are hard to find. It is clear that if one tries to stretch very little educational content out over an ever-longer period of time, dissatisfaction among the incarcerated is bound to increase and performance just as bound to decline. Also, if a broader and broader spectrum of the population weighted ever more heavily toward the working class is now required to take college entrance examinations

* *Editor's Note:* Another way in which the connection between IQ and sibling rank may be made is by arguing that first children receive more parental attention than second, and second more than third, etc. Therefore, because the environment is presumed to be richer for the earlier children than for the later ones the IQs of the earlier ones tend to be higher. The problem here, however, is that very little research has been done on the treatment of differently ranked siblings. Moreover, the variables include factors such as sex, spacing, and socioeconomic status, in addition to rank of sibling, and the effects of these are difficult to evaluate.

133

because it has become necessary to attend college and receive a diploma of some sort in order to gain the simplest prestigious jobs, then examination scores are sure to decline over time. The examinations are in part, of course, based in middle-class ideology.

It might be more interesting to simply consider schools in the context of the general decline in worker productivity in the United States for, nonmetaphorically, both teachers and students are the school workers and the scores are quality and quantity checks on the productivity of these workers. Such attempts at understanding these questions would have the virtue of seeing society as a whole.

Explanations along these lines seem obviously correct but they cannot be offered by bourgeois apologists or if offered they cannot be taken seriously, their implications followed out, etc., because these explanations are eventually destructive of the myths promulgated in capitalist society about education and its efficacy in leading one on to the good life.

Thus we conclude that the American educational system is rotten because the society from which it comes is rotten, built as it is on basic principles that lead people to exploit the labor and talents of others, indeed demand that exploitation, that celebrate the profit motive above all others, and that require the overwhelming and increasing majority of people to work at jobs destructive of mind and of body—all the while trying to accumulate an ever-greater pile of worthless goods, the only escape from the meaninglessness of work available. Some are not so lucky: they reside outside, a reserve labor force living a bare and despised and roller-coaster existence.[6]

Schools prepare people to accept society as it is, to defend it as it is against those few who would have it be different, or at least to believe that power and control—except in the narrow definition of these concepts offered in American electoral politics—are beyond them. Schools promote narrow competitiveness, petty individualism, acquisitiveness, personal/private self-satisfaction, etc. They are strange and unhappy places.

Things As They Could Be

But a society—this society—and consequently the educational system that naturally follows from it, could be quite differently organized and oriented.[7] Let us imagine a society in which everyone works cooperatively at maximizing the overall well-being of all; in which technical solutions are sought for handling dull, routine, and uninteresting work; in which technology is not used for destroying skill and separating thought from action for the sake of profit and production; in which, failing technical solution of the routine, such tasks are shared equally among all members of the society; in which people do not—indeed are not allowed to—want for the necessities of life, and luxuries in short supply and long demand are distributed by lot among those who desire them.[8]

In this society technology would be reined in in order to deal with the genuine and accumulated problems faced in the society; it would not engage in the fanciful and wasteful and destructive (actual and potential) pursuits that mark the technological "advances" of the United States. Thus decisions about what to do, what to produce, how and where to produce it, etc., would have to be made collectively with as wide popular participation as is possible and sensible. Thought and action, mind and body would act as one—the way "it 'spozed to be."[9]

Since, of course, such decisions would have to be informed and considered ones, the effective working of such a society would depend crucially on a well-educated population. Let us consider, then, what an educational system deriving as it would from a society organized along these general lines would have to be like. How sharply would it differ from our world?

Competitive educational practices would have to be replaced by cooperative ones: students would work together in the solution of problems and in the acquisition of knowledge; the fast would help and encourage the slow in their progress. Education would be a tough and demanding adventure.[10]

Education and work would also go ahead hand in hand. On this point, let us listen to Kropotkin once again:

> We do not want the educational process to act in the direction of dividing people, from childhood onward, into those who are led and those who lead, of whom the former are mainly familiar with the unskilled labor necessary for their daily lives—and the latter

mainly with the methods of management and the so-called higher manifestations of the human mind. . . .

Repeating the formulation of Proudhon, we say: if a naval academy is not itself a ship with sailors who enjoy equal rights and receive a theoretical education, then it will produce not sailors but officers to supervise sailors; if a technical academy is not itself a factory, not itself a trade school, then it will produce foremen and managers and not workmen, and so on. . . . In eliminating all the [un]necessary ballast of useless occupations, in devising accelerated methods of education (which always appear only when a demand for them arises which cannot be put off), the school will train healthy workers equally capable of both further intellectual and physical work.[11]

School years would not be years of being kept away from participating usefully in the work of the society and of then being finally allowed to engage in largely unnecessary labor. Schools would instead prepare people for a life of moving society ahead in solving its problems, reaching its goals. Indeed, in school there should begin a life of work and of play and of education that does not end with the conclusion of formal schooling.

Education in this sort of society would promote and develop the virtues of the society: cooperation, "mutual aid," concern for the well-being of one's comrades, etc. Thus both the form and the substance of education would necessarily be quite the opposite of what passes for education in our society.

But would or should such an education be devoted entirely to practical studies and to work, limited to a cooperative attack on the problems of production and distribution, to guaranteeing that nothing violates the basic equality of human relationships and rights, branching out into theoretical studies only when these contribute directly to the basic goals of society? Kropotkin seems to suggest that the answer to this question is yes, education should be so defined and limited. He would abolish the universities (in his day the center of theoretical studies, in fact limited to that) and confine to leisure time the pursuit of abstract studies for those who wished to spend their leisure time in that way.[12] Perhaps, but I do not believe this is necessary except in a society whose problems, accumulated through time (like those of the People's Republic of China or of Cambodia), are of such magnitude, so pressing, its available technology so minimal, that labor-intensive solutions are for the most part all that there is to turn to. However, in a society with advanced technological means all things can proceed simultaneously.

There is an even stronger argument in favor of not neglecting these theoretical studies, of including them in the education of us all: we must understand the species character and the species environment if we are to have a basis for a continually evolving revolution in a re-formed society.[13] Generation after generation the questions, Who are we? and Where are we?, must be asked and answered as fully as possible, without pretending that the answers are full and complete or that they lead on to solutions, products, etc. Indeed, it is one of the peculiarities of industrially advanced societies—capitalist or socialist—that theoretical studies must be bootlegged under the guise of their contributing directly to the solution of current problems. Theoretical studies are often also needed to justify the actions of the state so it can deal with its problems. In our re-formed society theoretical studies, scientific studies, would be a natural part of an education just as they are a natural part of man's cognitive capacity. It is to one aspect of these theoretical studies that I now turn.

Education As Explanation

It is a proper part of an education to enable students "to gain experience in constructing and articulating abstract, falsifiable explanations for superficially mysterious and contradictory observations."[14] Such enabling does not now occur to any great extent in our educational institutions because it and the present state of things could not coexist. Bill Ayers—now a member of the Weather Underground—observed this correctly in his discussion of the Children's Community school (in Ann Arbor):

> I mean, is it possible to have a lot of Children's Communities in this country?—and you start to throw that around. And what kind of kids will develop? and will they be able to fit into General Mo-

tors and a Ford plant? In evaluating questions like these, people may start to move, politically, at least in their heads. Because it is clear that the school system that now exists does a pretty good job of channeling people into different places, of fitting kids for the Ford factory and other kids for the executive offices, other kids for politics, and academics, whereas our system doesn't do that at all. Our system has, in that sense, a lot of very revolutionary implications because American society couldn't exist with a lot of Children's Communities, or said the other way, a lot of Children's Communities couldn't exist in America.[15]

But such enabling is a proper part of education and thus one of its necessary parts, perhaps its most necessary part, because insofar as the seemingly mysterious and contradictory observations are an examination of human nature, their explanation will provide insight into the human foundations for liberty.

In another place I have argued that an education must deal with matters for which there exist some reasonable attempts at explanation as well as with those for which the notion *explanation* seems forever to elude us.[16] This distinction is similar to the one that Chomsky has recently made between *problems* and *mysteries*.[17] The experience of engaging in explanation can only be gotten by looking at problems.

There are, of course, many problems that can be considered in this way and many mysteries to avoid or to look at in a different way with a different set of expectations, but the problems offering the most educational advantage—as far as I understand it—are those raised in the examination of language: through language we can look into the mind and out to the culture of which it is a part. Among the explanations of cognitive domains our understanding of language is sufficiently defined yet sufficiently open-ended to provide an area of discussion in which quite interesting and sophisticated observations can be made by naïve students and these then falsified, disconfirmed, confirmed, etc., all this without any great disrespect for the science or discipline involved. In this way it is superior for our purposes to the problems offered by the physical sciences, which often defy common-sense understanding and whose explanations depend on extending the senses.

For example, quite young children can recognize and organize the facts that underlie their recognition that another person is not a member of their speech community (of their geographic or social class dialect) and even provide a reasonable explanation of these facts.[18] They are able to give a pretty good account of the way in which animal communication systems and human language differ— something that students of primate behavior seem to have a great deal of trouble understanding sensibly. They can offer reasonable statements as to why we understand the subject of (1) "clean up that mess" to be "you" and how the relationships among the words of (2) "he is easy to please" and (3) "he is eager to please" differ. They can tell why (4) "Where do you want to go?," (5) "Where do you wanna go?," and (6) "Who do you want to go?" are possible but why (7) "Who do you wanna go?" is not.[19] They can explain the ambiguity of (8) "visiting relatives can be boring" and (9) "the police were ordered to stop drinking by midnight," and why it is reasonable to spell both *rejection* and *reject* with *t*'s in spite of the fact that the former unlike the latter does not contain the sound [t].[20] And so on for a wide range of facts about the sounds and sentences of the language, about the relationships between language and culture. Why, for instance, a white, lower-middle-class, Irish-Catholic teacher might say, "I don't understand you" to a child who has just said to him, "I ain't got none."

Students are able to integrate these one-by-one explanations into hypotheses about their "superficially mysterious and contradictory observations." All that is needed is a collective investigation of the language known by all the members of the class and a teacher who understands how to carry out a cooperative intellectual venture of this sort and who also understands the nature, state, and limits of the inquiry: the state of the explanation at any point in time. These are the crucial ingredients for explaining language phenomena.

In my own attempts to organize study of this sort—see the reference in footnote 18 and, inter alia, my introduction to N. R. Cattell's *The New English Grammar*[21]—I have always thought of the study as proceeding from very simple things to more complex matters: moving from, say, the structure of very simple sentences and phrases to an explanation of the structure of complex ones, from explanations of grammatical phenomena to explanations of sociolinguistic data. That is, you do not begin with the hardest things first, but *hardest* has to be defined in the context of an audience of children who do not necessarily find hard what adults find hard. For example, children evidently have little difficulty dealing with the intricacies of phonology and phonetics; adults do. The difference between (2) and (3), above, is lost on very young children. And so forth.

In any case, through a very carefully planned investigation of this sort there will arise a rational understanding of human differences as well as of particular characteristics of the human species. The relevance of this inquiry in American minority communities now— of inquiry into the nature of language and culture, of attempting to explain linguistic data—is that it serves to correctly legitimate what has in the past been impressed on these people as a burden, illegitimate baggage: their peculiar ways of speaking, of relating to one another, etc. If the naturalness of such things is in their examination laid bare, they then regain their proper stature. In a decent society the regaining of one's humanness would not be what any part of an education would be directed toward, but an understanding of it would be a vital and necessary part.

And once it is seen that mankind is to be studied as part of the natural universe and in just the same ways the rest of the universe is studied, it is then possible to expand outward to an examination of the world that surrounds us.[22] Language, because it is a mirror of the mind and a window on the world, is, I suggest, the best and easiest place to begin such studies. It opens up the rest.

REFERENCES

1. P. A. Kropotkin, *Selected Writing on Anarchism and Revolution,* edited by M. A. Miller (Cambridge: Massachusetts Institute of Technology Press, 1970), p. 47.

2. Essentially—in the area of higher education at least—the recommendations and wise counsel of the Carnegie Commission on Higher Education are being put into effect, and the consequences of this will soon be felt at the lower reaches of education.

3. See H. Braverman, *Labor and Monopoly Capital: The Degradation of Work in the Twentieth Century* (New York: Monthly Review Press, 1974),

pp. 435ff. See also the many essays of S. Bowles and H. Gintis, now integrated into their *Schooling in Capitalist America: Educational Reform and the Contradictions of Economic Life* (New York: Basic Books, 1976).

4. For fuller—though still preliminary—analyses of these matters, see my "Why *Newsweek* Can't Explain Things," in *Radical Teacher, a News Journal of Socialist Literary Theory and Practice*, no. 2, pp. 11-15 (available from the *RT* Business Office, P.O. Box 102, Cambridge, Mass. 02142) and my "Explaining Educational Failure" and "Explaining the Decline in SAT Scores" (both presently available in manuscript form from the author).

5. See R. Zajonc, "Dumber by the Dozen," *Psychology Today*, Jan., 1975; Susan Fogg, "Expert Blames Birth Order . . . ," *Boston Evening Globe*, Mar., 1, 1976. See, for similarly fanciful discussion of these matters, M. Sheils et al., "Why Johnny Can't Write," *Newsweek*, Dec. 8, 1975, pp. 58-65; UPI, "College-bound Youths Score Lower on Tests," *Boston Sunday Globe*, Jan. 15, 1976, p. 65; UPI, "Low SAT Scores Seen Tied to Elective Trend," *Boston Evening Globe*, Mar. 3, 1976, p. 4.

6. At the other end of the spectrum there are those who are trained to be leaders and managers and for them there exists a more or less separate system of education that performs these training functions, generally at the level of higher education, but often restricted to graduate education in the case of the managerial class. Note that we must be careful to restrict the class of managers to those who truly manage. Most white-collar workers are simply slaving away at tasks that are no more demanding than the ordinary assembly line job; they are, however, allowed to dress up for the occasion. See Braverman, *Labor and Monopoly Capital.*

7. Although an educational system is automatically entailed by the goals and social relationships characteristic of a society, it is possible for a successful political revolution to leave some of the institutions of the previous social order undisturbed. Thus in China a successful armed political revolution had to be followed nearly two decades later by the Great Proletarian Cultural Revolution, a revolution largely directed toward remaking the educational institutions, which had not changed significantly since the establishment of the People's Republic. See W. Hinton, *Hundred Day War: The Cultural Revolution at Tsinghua University* (New York: Monthly Review Press, 1972); and Edgar Snow, *The Long Revolution* (New York: Random House, 1972), among others.

8. "Facts" about human nature are often introduced at this point in discussions of this sort in order to argue that such things could not be, that what is exists because of these "facts"; however, since these "facts" do not indeed exist we shall say no more about them. See Noam Chomsky's "Toward a Humanistic Conception of Education," in W. Feinberg and H. Rosemont, eds., *Work, Technology, and Education* (Urbana: University of Illinois Press, 1975). See also his *Reflections on Language* (New York: Pantheon Books, 1976).

9. Innately? For an excellent discussion of questions of innateness, see Chomsky, *Reflections*, pp. 13ff.

10. See, for a discussion of what an education can and could be like, The Schoolboys of Barbiana, *Letter to a Teacher* (New York: Random House, 1970).

11. Kropotkin, *Selected Writings,* p. 58.

12. Kropotkin, *Selected Writings,* pp. 57ff.

13. See Chomsky, *Reflections,* pp. 132ff.

14. K. Hale and W. O'Neil, "A Proposal for a Masters Degree Program in Linguistics and Community Languages" (unpublished manuscript, 1975), p. 4.

15. B. Ayers, "Traveling with Children and Traveling On," in S. Repo, ed., *This Book Is about Schools* (New York: Pantheon Books, 1970), p. 351.

16. W. O'Neil, "Conference Report: Dartmouth Seminar," *Harvard Educational Review,* vol. 39, no. 2 (1969), pp. 359-65; and elsewhere.

17. Chomsky, *Reflections,* chap. 4, "Problems and Mysteries in the Study of Human Language."

18. See W. O'Neil, "A Report from Roxbury," scattered throughout W. C. Kvaraceus, ed., *Thirteen Professors Project: Episodes in Positive Teaching,* Project Report 5 (Washington, D.C.: NDEA National Institute for Advanced Study in Teaching Disadvantaged Youth, 1968).

19. N. Chomsky, "Conditions on Rules of Grammar," (unpublished manuscript, 1975), pp. 29ff and fn. 27. To make short work of a very complicated story, the fact that contraction cannot take place in (7) is related to the fact that the deep structure position of *who* is between *want* and *to go* for (6) and (7) while the deep structure position of *where* follows *to go* in (4) and (5).

20. For discussion of the rest of these briefly given examples see, for example, my introductory material on English orthography in the *American Heritage Dictionary of the English Language* and the discussion of my teaching experiences as described in "A Report from Roxbury."

21. N. R. Cattell, *The New English Grammar* (Cambridge: Massachusetts Institute of Technology Press, 1969), pp. ix-xvii.

22. Chomsky, *Reflections,* esp. chap. 1.

JERRY HIRSCH

Evidence for Equality: Genetic Diversity and Social Organization*

This essay is devoted to an examination of the evidence for equality. In keeping with the university's celebration of our nation's Bicentennial, I begin by considering the belief Thomas Jefferson inscribed in our Declaration of Independence: that it was "self-evident, that all men are created equal."

He worked assiduously to implement equality by removing inequity. In his autobiography Jefferson described how in the Virginia legislature he succeeded in abolishing the law of primogeniture (passing the family estate down to the firstborn son): "I proposed to abolish the law of primogeniture, and to make real estate descendible in parecenary to the next of kin, as personal property is, by the statute of distribution. Mr. Pendelton wished to preserve the right of primogeniture, but seeing at once that could not prevail, he proposed we should adopt the Hebrew principle, and give a double portion to the elder son. I observed, that if the eldest son could eat twice as much, or do double work, it might be a natural evidence of his right to a double portion; but being on a par in his powers and wants, with his brothers and sisters, he should be on a par also in the partition of the patrimony; and such was the decision of the other members."[1]

* Some of the ideas and parts of the discussion have been drawn from my papers: "Behavior Genetics and Individuality Understood: Behaviorism's Counterfactual Dogma Blinded the Behavioral Sciences to the Significance of Meiosis, *Science,* vol. 142 (1963), pp. 1436-42; "Behavior-Genetic, or 'Experimental,' Analysis: The Challenge of Science versus the Lure of Technology," *American Psychologist,* vol. 22, no. 2 (1967), pp. 118-30; "Behavior-Genetic Analysis and Its Biosocial Consequences," *Seminars in Psychiatry,* vol. 2 (1970), pp. 89-105.

The "Rough Draft" of the Declaration shows that Jefferson's belief in human equality derived from his ideas about creation: "We hold these truths to be sacred and undeniable; that all men are created equal and independent, *that from that equal creation* they derive rights inherent and inalienable . . . "[2] (italics added). Even though our understanding today of the details of creation is radically different from any beliefs Jefferson's contemporaries might have had about those details, it will be informative to compare the implications we can now draw with those that he drew.

I am going to consider the evidence for equality with respect to both our knowledge of genetic diversity and our knowledge of the relations between that genetic diversity and social organization. Fortunately, as you will now see, our understanding of genetic diversity in *no* way depends upon how we might define equality. Therefore, I can discuss the genetic situation first and worry about the meaning of equality later. Genes and chromosomes came before words and dictionaries.

It is no exaggeration to say that perhaps nothing in the history of science exceeds in richness and complexity the knowledge gained in this century both about the fundamental nature of heredity and about its multiform expressions throughout the living world. The last decade, however, has seen a series of misguided attempts to use, or rather to misuse, genetics in the explanation of the structure of society.

Understanding Individuality

The phenotype (appearance, structure, physiology, and behavior) of any organism is determined by the interaction of environment with its genotype (the complete genetic endowment). Each genotype is the end product of many mechanisms which promote genotypic diversity in populations.

Ordinarily, members of a cross-fertilizing, sexually reproducing species possess a diploid, or paired, set of chromosomes. Most species whose behavior we study are sexually dimorphic. The genetic basis of this dimorphism resides in the distribution of the heterosomes, a homologous pair of sex chromosomes (XX) being present in the mammalian female and an unequal pair (XY), in the mammalian male. Sexual dimorphism guarantees that any population will be variable to the extent of at least two classes. Whether sex-chromosome or other genotypic differences are involved in any particular behavior remains an empirical question to be investigated separately for every population. It can no longer be settled by dogmatic attitudes and assumptions about uniformity.

Chromosomes other than sex chromosomes are called autosomes. Every autosome is normally represented by a homologous pair whose members have identical genetic loci. Alternative forms of a gene any of which may occupy a given locus are termed alleles. If an individual receives identical alleles from both parents at homologous loci, he is said to be homozygous for that gene. If he receives two alleles that differ, however, he is said to be heterozygous for that gene. The process by which a gene changes from one allelic form to another is called mutation.

When a gene is represented in the population gene pool by two allelic forms, the population will be genotypically polymorphic to the extent of at least three classes. That is, individuals may be homozygous for either of two alleles or heterozygous for their combination.

Study of populations has revealed that often extensive series of alleles exist for a locus. Well-known examples are the three (actually more) alleles at the ABO-blood locus in man and a dozen or more alleles at the white-eye locus in *Drosophila*. In general, for each locus having n alleles in the gene pool, a population will contain $\frac{n(n + 1)}{2}$ genotypic classes. Mutation insures variety in the gene itself.

Sexual reproduction involves meiosis—a complex cellular process resulting in a meristic division of the nucleus and formation of gametes (reproductive cells) having single genomes (a haploid chromosome set). One homolog in every chromosome pair in our diploid complement is of paternal origin and the other is of maternal origin. In meiosis, the homologs of a pair segregate and a gamete receives one from each pair. The assortment to gametes of the segregating homologs occurs independently for each pair. This process insures diversity because it maximizes the likelihood that gametes will receive unique genomes. For example, gametogenesis in *Drosophila willistoni* produces eight alternative gametic genomes, which, if we represent the three chromosome pairs of this species by Aa, Bb, and Cc, we designate ABC, ABc, AbC, aBC, Abc, aBc, abC, abc (see fig. 1). In general, n pairs of chromosomes produce 2^n genomes (if we ignore the recombination of gene linkages that actually occurs in crossover exchanges between chromosomes). Man, with twenty-three chromosome pairs, produces gametes with any of 2^{23} alternative genomes. This makes vanishingly small the chances that even siblings (other than monozygotes) will be genetically identical. Since the gamete contributed by *each* parent is chosen from 2^{23} alternatives, the probability that the second offspring born to parents will have exactly the same genotype as their firstborn is $\left(\dfrac{1}{2^{23}}\right)^2$, or less than one chance in over 70 trillion! The probability that two unrelated individuals will have the same genotype, then, is effectively zero.

The argument for the genotypic uniqueness of members of populations is even more compelling, since other conditions also contribute to diversity.

The Abnormality of the Normal

Physiological systems are variable, not uniform (see figs. 2, 3, 4). Williams amply documents this and points out that implicit in our use of "normal" is reference to some region of a distribution arbitrarily designated as not extreme—for example, the median 50 percent, 95 percent, or 99 percent. We choose such a region for every trait. Among n mathematically independent traits—for example, traits dependent on n different chromosomes—the probability that a randomly selected individual will be normal for all n traits is the value for the size of that region raised to the nth power. Where "normal" is the median 50 percent and $n = 10$, on the average only one individual out of 1024 will be normal (for ten traits). When we consider at one time the distributions throughout a population of large numbers of physiological systems, we should expect negative deviates from some distributions to combine with positive deviates from others, both kinds of extreme deviates to combine with centrally located ones, and deviates of similar algebraic sign and magnitude to combine. Each individual's particular balance of physiological endowments will be the developmental

146

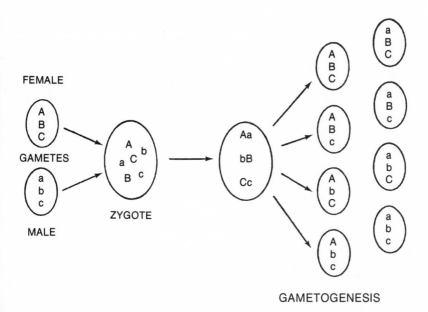

FIGURE 1. Recombination, segregation, and independent assortment. Maternal components (chromosomes or genes) in capital letters, paternal in lower case.

result of the genotype he draws in the lotteries of meiosis and the mating ritual. Because of crossing over, most genes assort independently. Hence, we cannot expect high correlations among the systems they generate.

If, underlying every behavior, there were only a single such system —for example, if the male "sexual drive" were mainly dependent on the seminal vesicles or if escape behavior were mainly dependent on the adrenals—then the same kind of distribution might be expected for both the behavior and the underlying system. Whatever uniformity might exist at one level would be reflected at the other. However, the last few decades of research on the biological correlates of behavior have made it increasingly clear that behavior is the integration of most of these systems rather than the expression of any one of them. Therefore, there is little reason to expect that the many possible combinations and integrations of those systems that go to make up the members of a population will

147

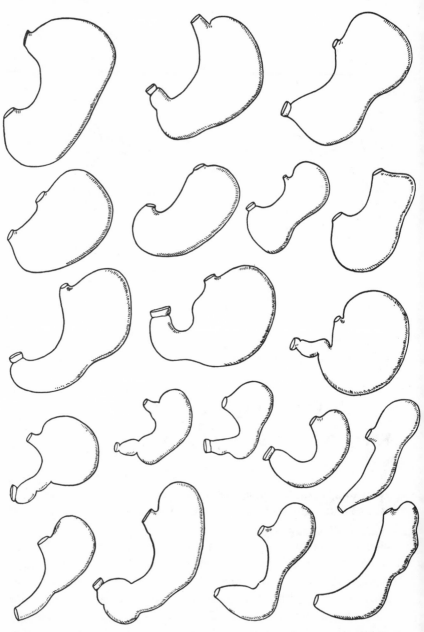

FIGURE 2. Stomach, variations in form. From laboratory specimens. (From R. J. Williams, *Biochemical Individuality*, John Wiley & Sons, New York, 1956, p. 21.)

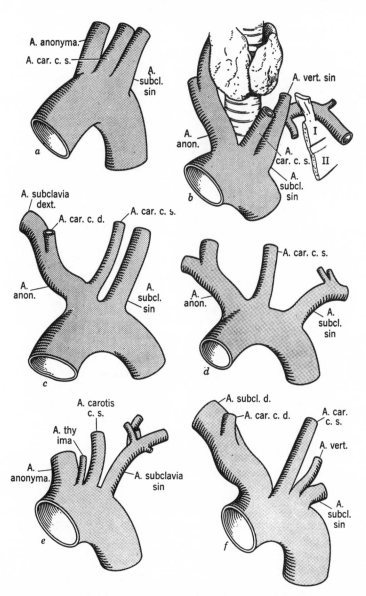

FIGURE 3. Branches of the aortic arch. Variation in the pattern of origin: a and b, common pattern; c and d, left common carotic artery from the innominate (long and short stem); e, separate origin of a thyreoidea ima artery; f, independent origin of a left vertebral. (From R. J. Williams, *Biochemical Individuality,* John Wiley & Sons, New York, 1956, p. 31.)

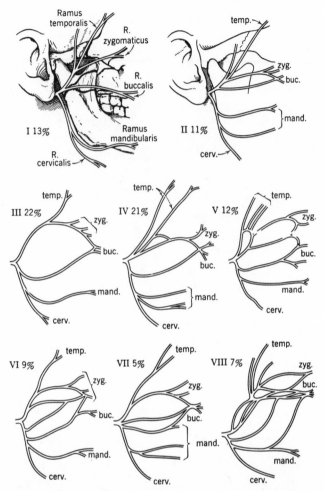

FIGURE 4. The facial nerve. Major types of facial nerve branching and anastomosis, with percentage occurrence (in 100 facial halves). I, Major divisions (temporal and facial) independent; II, anastomosis between rami of the temporal division; III, connection between adjacent rami from the major divisions; IV, anastomoses representing a composite of those in II and III; V, proximal anastomosis within the temporal component and distal interconnection between the latter and the cervical component; VI, two anastomotic rami sent from the buccal division of the cervical to the zygomatic part of the temporal; VII, transverse ramus, from the trunk of the nerve, contributing to the buccal ramus formed by anastomosis between the two major divisions; VIII, richly plexiform communications, especially within the temporal portion of the nerve. (From R. J. Williams, *Biochemical Individuality,* John Wiley & Sons, New York, 1956, p. 42.)

yield a homogeneously normal distribution of responses for many behavioral measures. An organism richly endowed with the components of one subset of systems and poorly endowed with those of another is not to be expected to behave in the same manner as an organism with an entirely different balance of endowments. The obviousness of this fact is well illustrated by the differences in behavior among the various breeds of dogs and horses.

Long ago the meaning of this diversity was accurately perceived and clearly stated by that outstanding biochemist Roger J. Williams in his genetotrophic principle: "Every individual organism that has a distinctive genetic background has distinctive nutritional needs which must be met for optimal well-being."[3] Of course, so much social behavior is devoted to our search for optimal well-being that there can be no question about our biosocial inequality, but this fact does not justify meritocratic fallacies involving superiority-inferiority hierarchies. It is to be expected that our diversity of needs and preferences must play an important role in our diversity of values.

Jefferson's intuition was superb. If we substitute meiosis and bisexual reproduction—nature's variation-generating probability mechanisms—for his "equal creation," we find that the mechanisms generating (creating) individuals are unbiased in the sense that an unlimited number of different types (individuals!) are possible and none are favored. Thus, that precious feature of democracy embodied in his idea of "equal creation" cannot be based on the nature of the individuals, who are uniquely different one from another, but rather on the unbiasedness of the system (meiosis and reproductive combinations) distributing genetic endowments. Note also that diversity provides the biological foundation for no enduring (elitist) hierarchy, only for an ever-shifting kaleiodoscopic variety of cultural arrangements.

Next, I shall consider "equality" before taking up evolution and population growth. Consultation of *The Oxford English Dictionary, Webster's Third International Dictionary,* and *Webster's New Dictionary of Synonyms* reveals that "equality" is defined as the condition of being equal in (1) quantity, amount, value, intensity, and other physical properties, (2) ability, achievement, excellence, and other psychological properties, and (3) quality, power, status, degree, and other sociopolitical properties; where "equal" means complete correspondence (such as in number, amount, magnitude, or value) and therefore equivalence but not selfsameness (which implies that the things considered are one and not two or more different things, i.e., identity). Thus, equality is defined as a condition prevailing among individuals who are different in the sense of being nonidentical, but who do not differ with respect to any measurable attribute—physical, psychological, sociopolitical, etc.—which, of course, is nonsense, because it is a contradiction. Equality and identity mean the same thing.

There is a fundamental difference between man and the other animal species. It lies in the medical and social statistics by which we proudly characterize the *progress* of our civilizations: declining infant mortality and declining mortality from an evergrowing list of diseases in an evergrowing list of nations; all of -this plus increased birth control, our protection from predation, and our taboos about killing.

Contrast the foregoing with the following facts: rodents (rats, mice, hamsters, etc.) of which there are over 300 genera and almost 3,000 species have litters varying in size from one or two up to fifteen or sixteen with an average below ten. Taking, for convenience, the number eight that we obtain in some of our mouse and rat colonies, we can calculate how a population might grow:

GENERATION	PARENTS	OFFSPRING	POPULATION
N_0		2	
N_1	2 ⟶	8	$8 + 2 = 10 = 5 \times 2$ pairs
N_2	10 ⟶	40	$40 + 10 = 50 = 25 \times 2$ pairs
N_3	50 ⟶	200	$200 + 50 = 250 = 125 \times 2$ pairs
N_4	250 ⟶	1000	$1000 + 250 = 1250 = 625 \times 2$ pairs
N_5			6250
N_6			31,250
N_7			156,250
N_8			781,250
N_9			3,962,500
N_{10}			19,812,500

in general:

$$N_t = N_0 (1 + p)^t$$

e.g., $N_{10} = 2 (1 + 4)^{10} = 19,812,500 \quad \approx \quad 20 \text{ million}$

Given good conditions they reach sexual maturity in a few weeks, closer to thirty than to sixty days, and gestation lasts only about twenty days, so it is possible to have over three generations a year and individuals can live two or more years. It is no exaggeration whatsoever to say that the reproductive capacity of a single couple might reach 20 million within the time of their own possible life span, because not only can their grandchildren be actively reproducing within the first year, but they themselves can have three or four litters in a year. Of course, it was precisely this insight transmitted by Malthus to both Darwin and Wallace which provided those two men with the key to evolution. Darwin even calculated that the slowest-breeding mammal, the elephant, would have produced 15 million descendants from a single couple in five centuries. The message of the Malthusian calculation is simple—the reproductive capacity of any species is sufficient to flood the planet, and yet none of them do. Selection pressure is intense. Only a small proportion of the possible progeny survive in each generation. That is, natural selection is eliminating diversity in prodigious quantities. It works to maintain a narrow fit to the available niche. Man in civilization, on the other hand, is doing ever more to limit reproduction and preserve the diversity and through technology is spawning an ever-increasing variety of cultural niches to accommodate his diversity. We are becoming maybe the most cosmopolitan species in the history of the animal kingdom. I have *not* claimed that human evolution has stopped, only that the pattern of selection pressures is no longer tailoring our species to a narrow niche of aggressive hunting and food gathering.

Much has been said about human diversity. Quite a bit of what has been said makes no reference to genes. Again, in keeping with our Bicentennial perspective, consider the following by our fourth President, James Madison, who contributed so much to the formulation of our Constitution:

> The diversity in the faculties of men, from which the rights of property originate, is . . . an insuperable obstacle to a uniformity of interests. The protection of these faculties is the first object of government. From the protection of different and unequal faculties of acquiring property, the possession of different degrees and kinds of

153

property immediately results; and from the influence of these on the sentiments and views of the respective proprietors ensues a division of the society into different interests and parties . . . . the most common and durable source of factions has been the various and unequal distribution of property. Those who hold and those who are without property have ever formed distinct interests in society. Those who are creditors, and those who are debtors, fall under a like discrimination. A landed interest, a manufacturing interest, a mercantile interest, a moneyed interest, with many lesser interests, grow up of necessity in civilized nations, and divide them into different classes, actuated by different sentiments and views. The regulation of these various and interfering interests forms the principal task of modern legislation and involves the spirit of party and faction in the necessary and ordinary operations of government.[4]

Genetic diversity has too often been interpreted to mean the genetic determination of individual differences in capacity to succeed—Social Darwinism in its most extreme form. Ironically, at the very moment when that virulent outbreak of racism known as Jensenism was being exposed as the hoax we now recognize it to be,[5] but which too many of our so-called intellectual elite failed to penetrate, a new and much more highly cultured voice began to be broadcast across the country. It spoke through the medium of an enormous volume with the title *Sociobiology: The New Synthesis* written by Harvard's Edward O. Wilson, published by Harvard with maximum publicity, and hailed in the popular press as thoroughly authoritative, just as were Jensen's misrepresentations in the immediately preceding years.

Wilson commands great respect, but so did the Nobel laureate Shockley and we now know how much nonsense he was capable of uttering.[6] Like his predecessor at Harvard, William Morton Wheeler, Wilson is recognized as having made valuable contributions to the study of the biology and of the sociology of ants. So his case is more complicated. It can best be understood in a historical perspective. First, however, let me summarize Wilson's very important arguments and then I shall explain the tradition into which we can fit so many of these events.

Wilson's Social Darwinian argument is simplicity itself: genetically different individuals are predisposed to play different roles in life—a fact which appears to be perfectly obvious to entomologists who study social insects having rigid caste systems. In Wilson's words, first about baboons and macaque monkeys and then about men:

> Insofar as . . . primate capabilities have a genetic basis—and there will almost certainly be some degree of heritability—the initial difference in developmental tendencies will be amplified into the striking divergence in status and roles that provide much of the social structure.[7]

> . . . open competition for leadership in an Indian community [Brazilian Yanomama] probably results in leadership being based far less on accidents of birth and far more on innate characteristics. . . . polygynous Indians, especially the headman, tend to be more intelligent. . . . also tend to have more surviving offspring.[8]

"In hunter-gatherer societies," Wilson observes, "men hunt and women stay home. This strong bias persists in most agricultural and industrial societies and, on that ground alone, appears to have a genetic origin." He then goes on to say: "My own guess is that the genetic bias is intense enough to cause a substantial division of labor in the most free and egalitarian of future societies."[9]

The extravagance of Wilson's exaggerations about man, a species for which evidence is unobtainable, can be evaluated in the light of his very incorrect account of the story of the fruit fly (*Drosophila melanogaster*), perhaps the most thoroughly studied metazoan species. In his eagerness to find experimental evidence for animal evolution actually observed in the laboratory, he presents a grossly distorted picture of the literature on this subject. When his distortions were challenged and he was confronted with the documentation for what was omitted from his account, i.e., that reliable evidence is nonexistent,[10] his retort was to make unsubstantiated charges that "political criteria were used to judge science."[11] So we now have at Harvard a politics of the success or failure to achieve and control evolution in the fruit fly experimentally in the laboratory. Recently, for his repeated defense of "bad science" by leveling indiscriminate charges of political motivation against critics exposing his faults, Wilson has earned this rebuke from Nobel laureate Sir Peter B. Medawar: "I believe it libellous to the point of being actionable to impute political motives to them."[12]

In order to appreciate this development we have to understand some of the history of people, places, and ideas. Edward O. Wilson was born and educated in our deep southern state of Alabama. He attended the University of Alabama where he earned both his bachelor's and master's degrees.[13] From there he went to Harvard to earn a Ph.D., and to rise to a professorship. Those of us who have been listening to Governor George Wallace over the years can understand how well an Alabama childhood and education might have prepared him for what he was to find at Harvard.

Wilson is Wheeler's intellectual successor at Harvard and Wheeler's influence on him is unmistakable. Wilson started at Harvard about 1950 and held a junior fellowship in its elite Society of Fellows (the organization Henderson worked so hard to found and then to shape) from 1953 to 1956. As the Evanses point out in their excellent life of Wheeler: "Wilson may be regarded as a 'second generation' student of Wheeler's, since he did his graduate work under F. M. Carpenter, a student of Wheeler's at the Bussey Institution who stayed to carry on the field of entomology at Harvard."[14] The power of Wheeler's influence is attested by no less than fifteen Wheeler references in *Sociobiology* and the absence there of any references at all to Carpenter.

Two of the most powerful intellectual influences on American thinking about biosocial science were professors and contemporaries at Harvard from the first decade of the century until about World War II: William Morton Wheeler (1865-1937) the entomologist (notoriously anti-Semitic in the Hitler era)[15] and Lawrence Joseph Henderson (1878-1942) the biochemist. While it would be unfair to claim that the influence I shall describe would not have been felt without Wheeler's initiative, it is a well-documented fact that Wheeler played a central role in bringing to the attention of America's intellectual community the work of a man who has been called the Karl Marx of fascism,[16] Vilfredo Pareto, a theoretician of economics and of sociology, whose ideas actually did influence early fascism. "In the summer of 1904 when Mussolini was living as a

draft evader in Switzerland, he enrolled for two of Pareto's courses
. . . at the University of Lausanne. . . ."[17] In 1923, shortly after
having seized power, Mussolini appointed Pareto to be a senator.
Mussolini later claimed Pareto as one of his intellectual masters.

These two intellectual giants, Wheeler and Henderson, made their
arguments for the importance of Pareto with a cogency that none
of their contemporaries seem to have been able successfully to
counteract. Like Pareto, Wheeler and especially Henderson in the
1930s, and now Wilson[18] have had as their goal to make sociology
a science. In Wheeler's words from one of *Sociobiology's* references,
which Wilson now echoes, this new approach was to "lift sociology
entirely out of the valuative and moralizing slough, in which it has
long floundered, onto the scientific plane. The strange light which
these and many other similar studies of human society cast on our
zealous social reformers and propagandists enables us to appreciate,
on the one hand, the impulsive, irrational, wishful thinking which
is the true drive of their own activities and, on the other hand, the
extraordinary magnitude and inertia of the behavior they are trying
to control and reform."[19]

Pareto was critical of Marxism and contributed to sociology a
theory of the circulation of elites, of social equilibria, and of the
importance of the irrational in behavior. However, I am not concerned here now with the details of Pareto's theory. What is important for us is his influence. His influential writings appeared in Italian and in French from the 1890s until his death in August, 1923.
In her excellent monograph *The Concept of Equilibrium in American Social Thought,* Cynthia Eagle Russett tells us:

> Despite a favorable review . . . Pareto's work did not generate
> much interest until Andrew Bongiorno and Arthur Livingston pub-
> lished a complete translation of the *Trattato,* entitled *The Mind
> and Society* in 1935. Thereupon . . . Pareto "burst like four Ro-
> man candles on the American sociological scene." And one of these
> candles appeared to have exploded just over the Charles: "for some
> reason, Harvard professors found the glow unusually attractive."
>
> The cause for Harvard's receptivity to the glow is not hard to find
> —a great deal of spadework had already been done there under the
> aegis of an extraordinary man, Lawrence Joseph Henderson, pro-

fessor of biological chemistry. . . . Henderson had been led to the French version of Pareto's work in 1928 by a colleague, William Morton Wheeler, whose study of insect societies had prompted him to take an interest in the structure of human society.[20]

As Russett explained: "The rationale for considering L. J. Henderson's work in detail is not only his stature as an intellectual figure of great intrinsic interest, bridging as he did the cultures of science and social theory, but the fact of his extraordinary influence on subsequent social science. . . . To a whole generation of Harvard students he passed on his conception of scientific method, of social science methodology, and specifically of the place of equilibrium analysis in social science."[21] Some of those who were strongly influenced by Henderson were: in anthropology Conrad Arensberg and Eliot D. Chapple, who later worked with Carleton S. Coon; in sociology George C. Homans and Talcott Parsons; in history Crane Brinton, Bernard De Voto, and Charles P. Curtis, the lawyer and legal historian; in business administration Wallace B. Donham, Elton Mayo, and Fritz Roethlisberger; and the businessman Chester I. Barnard, author of the classic organizational study *The Functions of the Executive.*

Therefore, it is no accident that misrepresentations about meritocracy (such as those by Herrnstein) and racism (as expressed by Jensen) once again found fertile soil at Harvard. Herrnstein dedicates his introductory text to S. S. Stevens, who weaned him from Skinner's environmentalism. Of course Stevens spent the entire decade of the 1930s on the scene at Harvard while Wheeler and Henderson were so actively promoting Pareto's elitism. (He had come from Stanford where "I absorbed the theory [= Jensenism] in evening seminars at the home of L. M. Terman, the father of the Stanford-Binet test."[22]) It was at that time that Stevens did the quantitative analyses for Sheldon's ectomorph-endomorph-mesomorph body typology. At this same time Shockley was near the Charles River at MIT.

The Achilles heel of the arch-hereditarian position, whether propounded by incompetents like Jensen and Herrnstein or by highly skilled specialists like Wilson, lies in their common failure to come to grips with a fundamental reality of development: the norm (or range) of reaction.

Norm of Reaction

The ontogeny of an individual's phenotype (observable outcome of development) has a norm or range of reaction not predictable in advance. In most cases the norm of reaction remains largely unknown; but the concept is nevertheless of fundamental importance, because it saves us from being taken in by glib and misleading textbook clichés such as "heredity sets the limits but environment determines the extent of development within those limits." Even in the most favorable materials only an approximate estimate can be obtained for the norm of reaction, when, as in plants and some animals, an individual genotype can be replicated many times and its development studied over a range of environmental conditions. The more varied the conditions, the more diverse might be the phenotypes developed from any one genotype. Of course, different genotypes should not be expected to have the same norm of reaction; unfortunately psychology's attention was diverted from appreciating this basic fact of biology by a half century of misguided environmentalism. Just as we see that, except for monozygotes, no two human faces are alike, so we must expect norms of reaction to show genotypic uniqueness. That is one reason why the heroic but ill-fated attempts of experimental learning psychology to write the "laws of environmental influence" were grasping at shadows. Therefore, those limits set by heredity in the textbook cliché can never be specified. They are plastic within each individual but differ between individuals. Extreme environmentalists were wrong to hope that one law or set of laws described universal features of modifiability. Extreme hereditarians were wrong to ignore the norm of reaction.

Individuals occur in populations and then only as temporary attachments, so to speak, each to particular combinations of genes. The population, on the other hand, can endure indefinitely as a pool of genes, maybe forever recombining to generate new individuals.

Ten years ago, before the latter-day hereditarians had gotten their bandwagon rolling, I closed an address to the American Psychological Association with the following remarks:

> I should like to point out certain trends that are now developing. As the social, ethnic, and economic barriers to education are removed throughout the world, and as the quality of education approaches a more uniformly high level of effectiveness, heredity may be expected to make an ever larger contribution to individual differences in intellectual functioning and consequently to success in our increasingly complex civilization. Universally compulsory education, improved methods of ability assessment and career counseling, and prolongation of the years of schooling further into the reproductive period of life can only increase the degree of positive assortative mating in our population. From a geneticist's point of view our attempt to create the great society might prove to be the greatest selective breeding experiment ever undertaken.
>
> Some might fear that this trend can only serve further to stratify society into a rigid caste system and that this time the barriers will be more enduring, because they will now be built on a firmer foundation. On the other hand, it may be noted that at least two conditions should prevent this from happening:
>
> 1. There is undoubtedly a significant contribution made to intellectual functioning by the unique organization of each individual's total genotype and by its idiosyncratic environmental encounters. Furthermore, mutation, recombination, and meiotic assortment, plus our inability to transmit more than a small part of individual experience as cultural heritage guarantee new variation every generation to produce the filial regression observed by Galton and to contribute to the social mobility discussed by Burt.[23]
>
> 2. The ever-increasing complexity of the social, political and technological differentiation of society creates many new niches (and abolishes some old ones) to be filled by each generation's freshly generated heterogeneity.[24]

The relation between heredity and behavior is one of neither independence nor isomorphism. Independence could have justified a naïve behaviorism, which might have studied "laws" of environmental influence on individuals who were fundamentally alike, i.e., the egalitarian argument would have been valid. Isomorphism might have tempted us into a Social Darwinian selectionist search for the *best types,* i.e., the eugenic-meritocratic arguments might have deceived us more easily. Neither one of the two extreme positions can be defended.

Genetic diversity is a fact of life, but there is no evidence that it produces recurrent types and can generate a social organization based on a caste hierarchy. In fact, as I showed at the outset, genetic reality guarantees that extremists at both ends of the heredity-environment spectrum will be frustrated. It is impossible for Social Darwinist eugenists to breed their ideal type. It is impossible for egalitarians to produce the conditions that will be equally good for, or satisfactory to, all individuals.

REFERENCES

1. Andrew A. Lipscomb and Albert Ellery Bergh, eds., *The Writings of Thomas Jefferson,* vol. 1 (Washington, D.C.: Thomas Jefferson Memorial Association, 1903), p. 64.

2. Gerald Force, compiler and designer, *The Jefferson Drafts of the Declaration of Independence in Facsimile* (Washington, D.C.: Acropolis Books, 1963), p. 3.

3. Roger J. Williams, *Biochemical Individuality* (New York: John Wiley & Sons, 1956), p. 167.

4. James Madison, *Paper No. 10,* in Clinton Rossiter, ed., *The Federalist Papers* (New York: Mentor Books, 1961), pp. 78-79.

5. Jerry Hirsch, "Jensenism: The Bankruptcy of 'Science' without Scholarship," *United States Congressional Record,* vol. 122: no. 73, E2671-2; no. 74, E2693-5; no. 75, E2703-5, E2716-8, E2721-2, 1976. (Originally published in *Educational Theory,* 1975, vol. 25, pp. 3-27.)

6. Mark Anthony, "Shockley Says Blacks Inferior; Meets Criticism," *The Lantern* (Ohio State University), vol. 94, no. 9 (Feb. 10, 1975), p. 1.

7. Edward O. Wilson, *Sociobiology: The New Synthesis* (Cambridge: The Belknap Press of Harvard University Press, 1975), p. 13.

8. Wilson, *Sociobiology,* p. 288.

9. Edward O. Wilson, "Human Decency Is Animal," *New York Times Magazine,* Oct. 12, 1975, pp. 48-50.

10. Jerry Hirsch, review of Edward O. Wilson's *Sociobiology: The New Synthesis, Animal Behaviour,* vol. 24 (1976), pp. 707-9.

11. Edward O. Wilson, reply to multiple reviews of *Sociobiology: The New Synthesis, Animal Behaviour,* vol. 24 (1976), pp. 716-18.

12. *New York Review of Books,* Mar. 31, 1977, p. 36.

13. Crane Brinton, ed., *The Society of Fellows* (Cambridge: The Society of Fellows of Harvard University, 1959), pp. 264-65.

14. Mary Alice Evans and Howard Ensign Evans, *William Morton Wheeler, Biologist* (Cambridge: Harvard University Press, 1970), p. 166.

15. Evans and Evans, *William Morton Wheeler*, p. 317.

16. R. V. Worthington, "The Karl Marx of Fascism," *Economic Forum*, vol. 1 (1933), pp. 311-15, 460-66.

17. H. Stuart Hughes, *Consciousness and Society* (New York: Vintage Books, 1958), p. 271.

18. Wilson, *Sociobiology;* Edward O. Wilson, "Academic Vigilantism and the Political Significance of Sociobiology," *BioScience*, vol. 26, no. 3 (1976).

19. W. M. Wheeler, "Social Evolution," in E. V. Cowdry, ed., *Human Biology and Racial Welfare* (New York: Hoeber, 1930), p. 154.

20. Cynthia Eagle Russett, *The Concept of Equilibrium in American Social Thought* (New Haven: Yale University Press, 1966), p. 111.

21. Russett, *Concept of Equilibrium*, p. 117.

22. S. S. Stevens, letter to the Editor, *The New York Times Magazine*, Sept. 28, 1969, p. 38.

23. Cyril Burt, "Intelligence and Social Mobility," *British Journal of Statistical Psychology*, vol. 14 (1961), pp. 3-24.

24. Jerry Hirsch, "Behavior-genetic, or 'Experimental,' Analysis," *American Psychologist*, vol. 22, no. 2 (1967), pp. 118-30.

NOAM CHOMSKY

Language Development, Human Intelligence, and Social Organization

I would like to comment on three notions of "equality": namely, equality of rights, equality of condition, and equality of endowment—and, more generally, the nature of that endowment, or, briefly, human nature and its variety. The last of these questions is essentially a matter of fact, one poorly understood but plainly in the domain of the natural sciences, and one to be answered, as best we can, by unprejudiced inquiry. The first two questions raise serious questions of value. All of these notions demand careful analysis, far beyond anything I can attempt here.

If the discussion of equality of rights and condition is to be at all serious—in particular, if it is to pertain to choice of action— then questions of fact inevitably intrude. Discussion becomes socially irrelevant, whatever interest it may retain as an intellectual exercise, to the extent that relevant facts are not accurately presented. In much current discussion of problems of equality, they are not accurately presented.

Consider, for example, a series of articles on egalitarianism by John Cobbs in *Business Week* (December, 1975), which is not untypical of current debate over these issues. Cobbs takes as his starting point the factual assumption that "in one way or another, all the government's social programs are equalizers" (although, he adds, federal programs do "not always achieve this result"). Does this factual premise even approximate the truth? A strong case can be made to the contrary. Subsidies to students for higher education, for example, tend to be roughly proportional to family income.

The enormous federal highway program has been in large measure a subsidy to commercial trucking (and, arguably, has indirectly raised the cost of living) and to major corporations that make their profits from petroleum and from modes of transportation that carry a substantial social cost. Nor can the government housing programs of the past thirty years be readily described as "equalizers." For example, the program in my own city destroyed "a low-income, predominantly Italian neighborhood" on Beacon Hill and replaced it with "high-income apartment towers financed with government-insured loans"—I quote from MIT Professor of Architecture Robert Goodman in a review of federal housing programs that he describes as an "effective way of exploiting the poor."[1] Or consider the government subsidies to arms producers and agribusiness, the latter, in part, through subsidy of research into agricultural technology, designed for the interests of large corporations, which is undertaken in government-supported universities. Or consider the vast government expenditures to insure a favorable international climate for business operations. In a highly inegalitarian society, it is most unlikely that government programs will be equalizers. Rather, it is to be expected that they will be designed and manipulated by private power for its own benefit; and to a significant degree this expectation is fulfilled. It is not very likely that matters could be otherwise in the absence of mass popular organizations that are prepared to struggle for their rights and interests. An effort to develop and implement government programs that really were equalizers would lead to a form of class war, and, in the present state of popular organization and distribution of effective power, there can hardly be much doubt about who would win—a fact that some "populists," who rightly deplore the government programs that benefit private economic power, sometimes tend to ignore.

Discussion of the role of the state in a society based on the principle of private power must not neglect the fact that "generally speaking, capitalism must be regarded as an economy of unpaid costs, 'unpaid' in so far as a substantial proportion of the actual costs of production remain unaccounted for in entrepreneurial outlays; instead they are shifted to, and ultimately borne by, third persons or by the community as a whole."[2] A serious analysis of the government's social programs—not to speak of its programs of economic intervention, military force, and the like—will assess the function of these programs in paying social costs that cannot realistically be relegated to a footnote. There may be a residual sense to the notion that the state serves as an equalizer, in that without its intervention the destructive forces of capitalism would demolish social existence and the physical environment, a fact that has been well understood by the masters of the private economy, who have regularly called upon the state to restrain and organize these forces. But the common idea that the government acts as a social equalizer can hardly be put forth as a general principle.

As a second example, consider the widely held doctrine that moves toward equality of condition entail costs in efficiency and restrictions of freedom. The alleged inverse relation between attained equality and efficiency involves empirical claims that may or may not be true. If this relation holds, one would expect to find that worker-owned and -managed industry in egalitarian communities is less efficient than matched counterparts that are privately owned and managed and that rent labor in the so-called free market. Research on the matter is not extensive, but it tends to show that the opposite is true.[3] Harvard economist Stephen Marglin has argued that harsh measures were necessary in early stages of the industrial system to overcome the natural advantages of cooperative enterprise, which left no room for masters, and there is a body of empirical evidence in support of the conclusion that "when workers are given control over decisions and goal setting, productivity rises dramatically."[4] From another point of view, Cambridge economist J. E. Meade has argued that efficiency and equitable distribution of income can be reconciled if measures are taken "to equalize the distribution of the ownership of private property and to increase the net amount of property which was in social ownership."[5] In general, the relation between equality and efficiency is hardly a simple or well-established one, despite many facile pronouncements on the matter.

Turning to the relation between equality and freedom, allegedly inverse, we also find nontrivial questions. Workers' control of production certainly increases freedom in some dimensions—extremely

important ones, in my judgment—just as it eliminates the fundamental inequality between the person compelled to sell his labor
power to survive and the person privileged to purchase it, if he so
chooses. At the very least, we should bear in mind the familiar
observation that freedom is illusion and mockery when conditions
for the exercise of free choice do not exist. We only enter Marx's
"realm of freedom" when labor is no longer "determined by necessity and mundane considerations,"[6] an insight that is hardly the
precept of radicals and revolutionaries alone. Thus Vico observed
that there is no liberty when people are "drowned . . . in a sea of
usury" and must "pay off their debts by work and toil."[7] David
Ellerman puts the issue well in an important essay:

> It is a veritable mainstay of capitalist thought (not to mention so-
> called "right-wing libertarianism") that the moral flaws of chattel
> slavery have not survived in capitalism since the workers, unlike the
> slaves, are free people making voluntary wage contracts. But it is
> only that, in the case of capitalism, the denial of natural rights is
> less complete so that the worker has a residual legal personality as
> a free "commodity-owner." He is thus allowed to voluntarily put
> his own working life to traffic. When a robber denies another per-
> son's right to make an infinite number of other choices besides los-
> ing his money or his life and the denial is backed up by a gun, then
> this is clearly robbery even though it might be said that the victim
> is making a "voluntary choice" between his remaining options.
> When the legal system itself denies the natural rights of working
> people in the name of the prerogatives of capital, and this denial
> is sanctioned by the legal violence of the state, then the theorists
> of "libertarian" capitalism do not proclaim institutional robbery,
> but rather they celebrate the "natural liberty" of working people
> to choose between the remaining options of selling their labor as a
> commodity and being unemployed.[8]

Considering such questions as these, we can hardly rest comfortably
with the assumption that freedom declines as equality—for example, in control over resources and means of production—increases.
It may be true that equality is inversely related to the freedom to
dispose of and make use of property under the social arrangements

of capitalism, but the latter condition is not to be simply identified as "freedom."

I do not even consider here the immeasurable loss incurred when a person is converted to a tool of production, so that, as Adam Smith phrased it, he "has no occasion to exert his understanding, or to exercise his invention . . . " and "he naturally loses, therefore, the habit of such exertion and generally becomes as stupid and ignorant as it is possible for a human creature to become . . . ," his mind falling "into that drowsy stupidity, which, in a civilized society, seems to benumb the understanding of almost all the inferior ranks of people."[9] What is the loss in "efficiency" and social product resulting from this enforced stupidity? What does it mean to say that a person driven to such "drowsy stupidity" by his conditions of work still remain "free"?

When we ask ourselves what would be a just and decent society, we are faced by conflicting intuitions, standards that are imprecise and poorly formulated, and significant questions of fact. Relying on some of these intuitions to the exclusion of others, we may seem to escape complexity and conflict, but at the risk of pursuing a mere logical exercise, and not a very interesting one at that. The hazards are well illustrated by some contemporary discussion. Consider, for example, the "entitlement theory of justice," which is now enjoying a certain vogue. According to this theory, a person has a right to whatever he has acquired by means that are just. If, by luck or labor or ingenuity, a person acquires such-and-such, then he is entitled to keep it and dispose of it as he wills, and a just society will not infringe on this right.

One can easily determine where such a principle might lead. It is entirely possible that by legitimate means—say, luck supplemented by contractual arrangements "freely undertaken" under pressure of need—one person might gain control of the necessities of life. Others are then free to sell themselves to this person as slaves, if he is willing to accept them. Otherwise, they are free to perish. Without extra question-begging conditions, the society is just.

The argument has all the merits of a proof that $2 + 2 = 5$. Presented with such a proof, we may be sufficiently intrigued to try to find the source of error in faulty reasoning or incorrect assumptions. Or we may disregard it and proceed to more important matters. In a field with real intellectual substance, such as mathematics, it may be interesting, and has in the past really proven fruitful, to pursue such questions. In considering the problems of society and human life, the enterprise is of dubious value. Suppose that some concept of "just society" is advanced that fails to characterize the situation just described as unjust, to an extreme (however the outcome may have come about). Then one of two conclusions is in order. We may conclude that the concept is simply unimportant and of no interest as a guide to thought or action, since it fails to apply properly even in such an elementary case as this. Or we may conclude that the concept advanced is to be dismissed in that it fails to correspond to the pre-theoretical notion it intends to capture in clear cases. If our intuitive concept of justice is clear enough to rule social arrangements of the sort described as grossly unjust, then the sole interest of a demonstration that this outcome might be "just" under a given "theory of justice" lies in the inference, by *reductio ad absurdum,* to the conclusion that the theory is hopelessly inadequate. While it may capture some partial intuition regarding justice, it evidently neglects others.

The real question to be raised about theories that fail so completely to capture the concept of justice in its significant and intuitive sense is why they arouse such interest. Why are they not simply dismissed out of hand on grounds of this failure, which is so striking in clear cases? Perhaps the answer is, in part, the one given by Edward Greenberg in a discussion of some recent work on the entitlement theory of justice. After reviewing empirical and conceptual shortcomings, he observes that such work "plays an important function in the process of . . . 'blaming the victim,' and of protecting property against egalitarian onslaughts by various non-propertied groups."[10] An ideological defense of privilege, exploitation, and private power will be welcomed by some, regardless of its merits.

These matters are of no small importance to poor and oppressed people here and elsewhere. Forms of social control that sufficed to insure obedience in an expanding economy have lost their efficacy in times of stagnation. Ideas that circulate in the faculty club and executive suite can be transmuted into ideological instruments to confuse and demoralize. Furthermore, in 1976 we can hardly ignore the fact that the power of the American state has been employed, on a massive scale, to impose capitalist social forms and ideological principles on unwilling and resisting victims throughout the world. Academic ideologists and political commentators in the media may choose to interpret history in other terms, but the business press is considerably more accurate in observing that the "stable world order for business operations," "the international economic structure, under which U.S. companies have flourished since the end of World War II," has been dependent on the organized violence of the state: "No matter how negative a development, there was always the umbrella of American power to contain it," though in the world after Vietnam, they fear, "this may no longer be so."[11]

I once visited a village in Laos in the middle of which there was a pleasant lake that had, at one time, served as the water supply for the village and a place where villagers could relax and enjoy themselves. One powerful individual had succeeded in gaining control of all access to the lake, now fenced off. To obtain water, villagers had to trudge several miles. They could see the lake beyond the fence, but it was no longer available to them. Suppose that ownership of that lake had been attained by means that were "just," as certainly might have been the case in principle.[12] Would we then conclude that the village was a "just society," in this respect? Would we seriously urge the villagers to accept this consequence, as only right and just? The government backed—it would be more accurate to say imposed—by the United States implicitly took that position. The Pathet Lao organized the peasants of Laos to overcome such forms of "justice." So substantial was their success that the U.S. government undertook to demolish much of rural Laos in a war that was "secret," in that the free press in our free society freely chose to keep it secret for a long period while thousands of peasants were murdered and dispossessed. We now freely choose to forget what has happened and erase it from history, or to dismiss it as an unfortunate though minor incident, an example of our "blundering efforts to do good," our "good intentions" mysteriously transmuted into "bad policy" through our ig-

169

norance, error, and naïveté.[13] In fact, the question of "justice" in crucial cases such as this one is by no means abstract and remote, and we would do well to think seriously about it.

Similar questions arise in a stark form in our own society, one that has a substantial degree of freedom by world standards. For example, we have free access to information, in principle. In the case of the secret war in Laos, it was possible to ascertain the facts —much too late—by visiting the country, speaking to people in refugee camps, and reading reports in the foreign press and ultimately even our own. But freedom of that sort, though important for the privileged, is socially rather meaningless. For the mass of the population of the United States, there was no opportunity, in the real world, to gain access to that information, let alone to comprehend its significance. The distribution of power and privilege effectively limits the access to information and the ability to escape the framework of doctrine imposed by ideological institutions: the mass media, the journals of opinion, the schools and universities. The same is true in every domain. In principle, we have a variety of important rights under the law. But we also know just how much these mean, in practice, to people who are unable to purchase them. We have the right of free expression, though some can shout louder than others, by reason of power, wealth, and privilege. We can defend our legal rights through the courts— insofar as we understand these rights and can afford the costs. All of this is obvious and hardly worth extended comment. In a perfectly functioning capitalist democracy, with no illegitimate abuse of power, freedom will be in effect a kind of commodity; effectively, a person will have as much of it as he can buy. We readily understand why the powerful and the privileged often rise to the defense of personal freedom, of which they are the chief beneficiaries in practice, though they manage to look the other way when, for example, the national political police become involved in political assassination and destruction of political groups that attempt to organize among the poor, as happened in Chicago not very long ago to the resounding silence of the national press and journals of opinion.[14]

I have only barely touched on some of the questions that arise when we consider problems of equality and freedom. I have as yet said nothing at all about the third notion of equality, namely, "equality of endowment." Here, too, there is a widely held doctrine that deserves examination. Again, it is expressed clearly by John Cobbs. He poses what he takes to be "the great intellectual dilemma of the egalitarians," namely, that "a look at the real world demonstrates that some men are smarter than others." Is it fair to insist, he asks, that "the fast and the slow . . . should all arrive at the same condition at the same time?" Is it fair to insist on equality of condition achieved, when natural endowment so plainly varies?

Presumably, it is the case that in our "real world" some combination of attributes is conducive to success in responding to "the demands of the economic system." Let us agree, for the sake of discussion, that this combination of attributes is in part a matter of native endowment. Why does this (alleged) fact pose an intellectual dilemma to egalitarians? Note that we can hardly claim much insight into just what the relevant combination of attributes may be. I know of no reason to believe, and do not believe, that "being smart" has much to do with it. One might suppose that some mixture of avarice, selfishness, lack of concern for others, aggressiveness, and similar characteristics play a part in getting ahead and "making it" in a competitive society based on capitalist principles. Others may counter with their own prejudices. Whatever the correct collection of attributes may be, we may ask what follows from the fact, if it is a fact, that some partially inherited combination tends to lead to material success. All that follows, so far as I can see, is a comment on our particular social and economic arrangements. One can easily imagine a society in which physical prowess, willingness to murder, ability to cheat, and so on, would tend to bring success; we hardly need resort to imagination. The egalitarian might respond, in all such cases, that the social order should be changed so that the collection of attributes that tends to bring success will no longer do so. He might even argue that in a more decent society the attributes that now lead to success would be recognized as pathological, and that gentle persuasion might be a proper means to help people to overcome their unfortunate malady. Again we return to the question, What is a just and decent social order?

The egalitarian faces no special intellectual dilemmas distinct in character from those that confront the advocates of a different social order.

A standard response is that it is just "human nature" to pursue power and material interest by any means so long as one can get away with it. Let us suppose that human nature is such that under given social conditions these admirable traits manifest themselves, or, more accurately, that people with such tendencies will prosper. Suppose further that wealth and power, once attained, can be employed to extend and protect such privilege, as has been the case under industrial capitalism. The obvious question, of course, is whether other social arrangements might be brought into being that would not encourage these tendencies but would rather be conducive to the flourishing of other traits that are no less part of our common nature: solidarity, concern, sympathy, and kindness, for example.

Discussion of egalitarian views is often misleading, in that the criticism of such views is commonly directed against a straw-man opponent, as egalitarians have been quick to point out.[15] In fact, "equality of condition," much deplored by contemporary ideologists, has rarely been the express goal of reformers or revolutionaries, at least on the left. In Marx's utopia, "the development of human energy" is to be taken as "an end in itself" as humans escape the "realm of necessity" so that questions of freedom can be seriously raised. The guiding principle, reiterated to the point of cliché, is: "From each according to his abilities, to each according to his needs." The principle of "equality of condition" is nowhere invoked. If one person needs medical treatment and another is more fortunate, they are not to be granted an equal amount of medical care, and the same is true of other human needs.

Libertarian socialists who objected to the theory of proletarian dictatorship also saw little merit in "egalitarianism" as such and in fact condemned "authoritarian socialism" for failing to comprehend that "Socialism will be free or it will not be at all":

> In the prison, in the cloister, or in the barracks one finds a fairly high degree of economic equality, as all the inmates are provided

with the same dwelling, the same food, the same uniform, and the same tasks. The ancient Inca state in Peru and the Jesuit state in Paraguay had brought equal economic provision for every inhabit- `
ant to a fixed system, but in spite of this the vilest despotism pre-
vailed there, and the human being was merely the automaton of a
higher will on whose decisions he had not the slightest influence.
It was not without reason that Proudhon saw in a "Socialism" without freedom the worst form of slavery. The urge for social justice
can only develop properly and be effective when it grows out of
man's sense of freedom and responsibility, and is based upon it.[16]

For Rocker, anarchism was "voluntary socialism" and "freedom
is not an abstract philosophical concept, but the vital concrete possibility for every human being to bring to full development all capacities and talents with which nature has endowed him, and turn them
to social account." Marx would not have disagreed, and the basic
conceptions can be traced back to earlier libertarian thought.[17]
These ideas deserve close attention as the most serious expression,
in my view, of a concept of a just and decent society that incor-
porates serious and critical principles while attending to significant
social and historical facts.

Note that for such socialists as Marx, Bakunin, Rocker, and
others of the left, there is no "intellectual dilemma" arising from
inequality of endowment. Libertarian socialists, at least, looked
forward to "a federation of free communities which shall be bound
to one another by their common economic and social interests and
arrange their affairs by mutual agreement and free contract," "a
free association of all productive forces based upon co-operative
labor, which would have for its sole purpose the satisfying of the
necessary requirements of every member of society."[18] In such a
society, there is no reason why rewards should be contingent on
some collection of personal attributes, however selected. Inequality
of endowment is simply the human condition—a fact for which
we may be thankful; one vision of hell is a society of interchange-
able parts. It carries with it no implications concerning social
rewards.

In a socialist society, as envisioned by the authentic left,[19] a central purpose will be that the necessary requirements of every mem-

ber of society be satisfied. We may assume that these necessary requirements will be historically conditioned in part and will develop along with the expansion and enrichment of material and intellectual culture. But "equality of condition" is no desideratum, as we appproach Marx's "realm of freedom." Individuals will differ in their aspirations, their abilities, and their personal goals. For some person, the opportunity to play the piano ten hours a day may be an overwhelming personal need; for another, not. As material circumstances permit, these differential needs should be satisfied in a decent society, as in healthy family life. In functioning socialist societies such as the Israeli kibbutzim, questions of this sort constantly arise. I cannot imagine that it is possible to formulate very strong general principles to resolve conflicts and measure individual opportunity against social demands. Honest people will differ in their assessments and will try to reach agreement through discussion and sympathetic consideration of the needs of others. The problems are not exotic ones; they arise constantly in functioning social groups such as the family. We are not accustomed to thinking beyond such small groups, given the inhuman and pathological premises of competitive capitalism and its perverse ideology. It is no wonder that "fraternity" has traditionally been inscribed on the revolutionary banner alongside "liberty" and "equality." Without bonds of solidarity, sympathy, and concern for others, a socialist society is unthinkable. We may only hope that human nature is so constituted that these elements of our essential nature may flourish and enrich our lives once the social conditions that suppress them are overcome. Socialists are committed to the belief that we are not condemned to live in a society based on greed, envy, and hate. I know of no way to prove that they are right, but there are also no grounds for the common belief that they must be wrong.

The distinction between equality of condition and equality of rights loses its apparent sharpness when we attend to it more closely. Suppose that individuals, at each stage of their personal existence, are to be accorded their intrinsic human rights; in this sense, "equality of rights" is to be upheld. Then conditions must be such that they can enjoy these rights. To the extent that inequality of condition impairs the exercise of these rights, it is illegitimate and is to be overcome, in a decent society. What then are these rights? If they include the right to develop one's capacities to the fullest, to realize what Marx calls the "species character" of "free conscious activity" and "productive life" in free associations based on constructive, creative work, then conditions must be equalized at least to the rather considerable extent required to guarantee these rights, if equality of rights is to be maintained. The vision of the left, then, blurs the distinction between equality of rights and equality of condition, denies that inequality of endowment merits or demands corresponding inequality of reward, rejects equality of condition as a principle in itself, and sees no intellectual dilemma in the conflict between egalitarian principles, properly understood, and inequality of endowment. Rather, we must face the problems of a repressive and unjust society, which emerge with greater clarity as we approach the realm of freedom.

Criticisms of egalitarianism misfire when directed against at least this segment of the left. But one may legitimately raise other questions. Thus it might be argued that the intuitions that lead to this vision of a decent and just society conflict with others: for example, the belief that one must pay for one's sins or errors. Or it might be argued that all of this is utopian nonsense, and that wage slavery and authoritarian structures such as the modern business enterprise are an inescapable necessity in a complex society. Or one may consider a more limited time frame and work for "more equality" and "more justice," putting aside the question of further goals and the principles that inspire them. Here we enter the grounds of legitimate and useful controversy. For example, if an argument can be constructed that advanced industrial societies cannot survive unless some people rent themselves to others, some people giving orders while others march to the beat of a drum, then it should be taken seriously. If correct, it undermines the socialist vision. But the burden of proof rests on those who insist that some fundamental conditions of repression, exploitation, or inequality are inescapable. To say merely that things have never been otherwise is not very convincing. On these grounds, one could have demonstrated in the eighteenth century that capitalist democracy is an impossible dream.

Can we seriously raise the question, what is human nature? Can we make some progress toward the understanding of human nature? Can we develop a theory of intrinsic human needs, of the nature of human capacities and their variation in the species, of the forms these capacities will assume under varied social conditions, a theory that will have some consequences or at least be suggestive with regard to questions of human and social import? In principle, we enter at this point into the domain of scientific inquiry, although it is potential rather than actual science.

The proposition that humans differ in fundamental respects from other organisms in the natural world is hardly open to serious dispute. If a Martian scientist were to study earthly matters, he would have little doubt on this score. The conclusion would be particularly obvious if he were to observe changes in the lives of organisms over an extended period. The humans of today are, with at most minor modifications, of the same genetic constitution as their forebears many millenia ago, but patterns of life have changed remarkably, particularly in the past few hundred years. This is not true of other organisms, except as a result of human intervention. A Martian observer would also be struck by the fact that at any moment of history there are remnants of earlier ways, even of Stone Age conditions, among humans who do not differ significantly in genetic constitution from those whose mode of life has changed most radically. He would note, in short, that humans are unique in the natural world in that they have a history, cultural diversity, and cultural evolution. In these respects, our hypothetical Martian might well be intrigued by the question, Why is this so?

The same question has, of course, been raised in one or another form since the earliest recorded origins of human thought. That is natural enough. Humans naturally seek to define their place in the world of nature. The question, What is human nature, the collection of attributes that so radically distinguish the human species from the rest of the organic world, is a profound and essentially unanswered question of science. It has been held to lie beyond the range of scientific inquiry, in that the specific difference of humans lies in their possession of an immortal soul that cannot be further understood by the methods of science. We might note that the inaccessibility of the soul to study is no essential conclusion of dualist theory. One might argue, say on Cartesian grounds, that humans and humans alone possess some nonmaterial quality— the Cartesian mind; and yet one might maintain, as some Cartesians might have agreed, that there can be a science of mind. But putting this issue aside, there are quite unique properties of human intelligence, elements of distinctive human nature. Assuming no a priori limits to inquiry, it is an empirical question, a question of science, to determine what human nature may be.

The puzzlement of our hypothetical Martian observer, with regard to the uniqueness of the human species, would perhaps mount if he knew a little modern biology. Thus it seems to be the case that the quantity of DNA in the fertilized egg is not very different for a mouse, a cow, a chimpanzee, or a person. Structural differences revealed only at a more refined level of analysis are evidently responsible for the precise course and character of embryological development. In a complex and intricate system, small differences in initial condition may have major consequences for the form, size, structure, and function of the resulting organism and its components. The same phenomenon is commonplace in the natural sciences. It can also be easily demonstrated in the investigation of a system of the intricacy of human language. Given a linguistic theory of sufficient range and complexity, it is easy to show that small modifications in general conditions imposed on rules may lead to very curious and varied changes among predicted phenomena, because of the complex interactions that take place as a sentence is generated by a system of rules operating under these conditions. Assuming that modern biology is essentially on the right track, it must be that natural selection gave rise somehow to a particular quality of genetic complexity, producing "a new force: the human mind," a "unique instrument [that] gave for the first time to a biological species the power to alter its relation to the environment . . . by conscious manipulation of the surrounding world" as well as the means for expression of thought and emotion, for creation of art and science, for planning actions and assessing their consequences over a hitherto inconceivable range. It is often assumed, quite plausibly, that in the development of this unique instrument, the human mind, "the critical step must have been the invention of language."[20] In some manner that is still poorly understood, genetic endowment was modified to produce a creature that grows a human language as part of a system of "mental organs," a creature that can then proceed to create the conditions under which it will live to an extent without significant analog so far as we know.

The question what is human nature has more than scientific interest. As we have noted, it lies at the core of social thought as well. What is a good society? Presumably, one that leads to the satisfaction of intrinsic human needs, insofar as material conditions allow. To command attention and respect, a social theory should be grounded on some concept of human needs and human rights, and, in turn, on the human nature that must be presupposed in any serious account of the origin and character of these needs and rights. Correspondingly, the social structures and relations that a reformer or revolutionary seeks to bring into existence will be based on a concept of human nature, however vague and inarticulate.

Suppose that at the core of human nature lies the propensity to truck and barter, as Adam Smith alleged. Then we will work to achieve an early capitalist society of small traders, unhindered by monopoly, state intervention, or socially controlled production. Suppose, in contrast, that we take seriously the concepts of another classical liberal thinker, Wilhelm von Humboldt, who contends that "to inquire and to create—these are the centers around which all human pursuits more or less directly revolve," and who further maintains that true creation can take place only under conditions of free choice that goes beyond "instruction and guidance," in a society in which social fetters have been replaced by freely created social bonds. Or suppose that we assume further with Marx that "only in a state of community with others has each individual the means to develop his predispositions in all directions; only in a state of community will personal freedom thus become possible" —where personal freedom presupposes abolition of the alienation of labor that Humboldt condemned as well, the condition of labor that "casts some of the workers back into a barbarous kind of work and turns others into machines."[21] On such assumptions about human needs, we derive a very different conception of a social order that we should work to create.

Some Marxists have taken the view that "man has no essence apart from his historical existence,"[22] that "human nature is not something *fixed by nature,* but, on the contrary, a 'nature' which is *made by man* in his acts of 'self-transcendence' as a natural being."[23] This interpretation derives from Marx's dictum that "the nature which comes to be in human history—the genesis of human society —is man's real nature"[24] and other similar remarks. Even if we adopt this view, it still remains true that the next step in social change should seek to provide the conditions for the "real nature" that can be expressed at a given stage of historical and cultural evolution.

Is it true that human nature is in no way "fixed by nature"? Evidently it is not true of the physical components of human nature. When a modern Marxist thinker such as Antonio Gramsci, for example, argues that "the fundamental innovation introduced by Marxism into the science of politics and history is the proof that there does not exist an abstract, fixed and immutable 'human nature' . . . but that human nature is the totality of historically determined social relations,"[25] he is referring, of course, not to human physical organs in general but to one specific organ, the human brain and its creations. The content of this doctrine must be that at least so far as the higher mental functions are concerned, the human brain is unique among the systems known to us in the natural world in that it has no genetically determined structure, but is, in effect, a *tabula rasa* on which the totality of historically determined social relations is then inscribed. For some segments of the left, there has been an extraordinary compulsion to adopt some such view. In a report on a recent discussion at the American Association for the Advancement of Science, Walter Sullivan writes: "The most extreme view, expressed by some members of the audience, was that human brains were 'uncoupled' from any genetic influences whatsoever—that, like computers built to a standard design, their relative levels of performance were completely determined by programming."[26]

As scientific hypotheses, these assumptions, which are familiar from radical behaviorism as well, seem to me to have very little to recommend them. On these assumptions, it would be quite impossible to account for the richness and complexity of human cognitive systems and the uniformity of their growth, not to speak of the remarkable qualitative differences as compared with other species. Surely no evidence or argument has been adduced in support of the belief that the human brain is markedly distinct from every other structure known to us in the natural world, and it is perhaps a bit ironic that such views are proposed, not only on the left, as if they were an outgrowth of some kind of scientific naturalism. Exactly the contrary seems to me to be the case. The human brain is unique in many respects, and the mental structures that grow under the boundary conditions set by experience—the cognitive structures that are "learned," to employ the common and I think rather misleading locution—also provide humans with a "unique instrument." But it is difficult to imagine that this "uniqueness" resides in the absence of structure, despite the antiquity of such a belief and its remarkable grip on the modern imagination. What little we know about the human brain and about human cognitive structures suggests a very different assumption: a highly constrained genetic program determines the basic structural properties of our "mental organs," thus making it possible for us to attain rich and intricate systems of knowledge and belief in a uniform manner on the basis of quite limited evidence. I might add that such a view comes as no surprise to biologists, particularly, as regards human language.[27] And I believe it would generally be regarded by neurophysiologists as entirely natural, if not almost obvious.

We need not rest with qualitative and vague remarks such as these. In the study of human language, at least, there are substantive hypotheses, which I believe have considerable force and explanatory power, about the general character of the genetic program that provides for the growth of the capacity for language and the particular forms that it assumes. I see no reason to doubt that the same will prove true in other domains, as we come to understand the structure of human cognitive capacity. If so, we may think of human nature as a system of a sort familiar in the biological world: a system of "mental organs" based on physical mechanisms that are now largely unknown, though not beyond investigation in principle, a system that provides for a unique form of intelligence

180

that manifests itself in human language, in our unique capacity to develop a concept of number and abstract space,[28] to construct scientific theories in certain domains, to create certain systems of art, myth, and ritual, to interpret human actions, to develop and comprehend certain systems of social institutions, and so on.

On an "empty organism" hypothesis, human beings are assuredly equal in intellectual endowments. More accurately, they are equal in their incapacity to develop complex cognitive structures of the characteristically human sort. If we assume, however, that this biologically given organism has its special capacities like any other, and that among them are the capacities to develop human cognitive structures with their specific properties, then the possibility arises that there are differences among individuals in their higher mental functions. Indeed, it would be surprising if there were not, if cognitive faculties such as the language faculty are really "mental organs." People obviously differ in their physical characteristics and capacities; why should there not be genetically determined differences in the character of their mental organs and the physical structures on which they are based?

Inquiry into specific cognitive capacities such as the language faculty leads to specific and I think significant hypotheses concerning the genetically programmed schematism for language, but gives us no significant evidence concerning variability. Perhaps this is a result of the inadequacy of our analytic tools. Or it may be that the basic capacities are truly invariant, apart from gross pathology. We find that over a very broad range, at least, there are no differences in the ability to acquire and make effective use of a human language; at some level of detail, there may be differences in what is acquired, as there are evidently differences in facility of use. I see no reason for dogmatism on this score. So little is known concerning other cognitive capacities that we can hardly even speculate. Experience seems to support the belief that people do vary in their intellectual capacities and their specialization. It would hardly come as a surprise if this were so, assuming that we are dealing with biological structures, however intricate and remarkable, of known sorts.

Many people, particularly those who regard themselves as within the left-liberal political spectrum, find such conclusions repugnant. It may be that the empty organism hypothesis is so attractive to the left in part because it precludes these possibilities; there is no variability in a null endowment. But I find it difficult to understand why conclusions of this sort should be at all disturbing. I am personally quite convinced that no matter what training or education I might have received, I could never have run a four-minute mile, discovered Gödel's theorems, composed a Beethoven quartet, or risen to any of innumerable other heights of human achievement. I feel in no way demeaned by these inadequacies. It is quite enough that I am capable, as I think any person of normal endowments probably is, of appreciating and in part understanding what others have accomplished, while making my own personal contributions in whatever measure and manner I am able to do. Human talents vary considerably, within a fixed framework that is characteristic of the species and that permits ample scope for creative work, including the creative work of appreciating the achievements of others. This should be a matter for delight rather than a condition to be abhorred. Those who assume otherwise must be adopting the tacit premise that a person's rights or social reward are somehow contingent on his abilities. As for his rights, there is an element of plausibility in this assumption in the single respect already noted: in a decent society opportunities should conform as far as possible to personal needs, and such needs may be specialized and related to particular talents and capacities. My pleasure in life is enhanced by the fact that others can do many things that I cannot, and I see no reason to want to deny these people the opportunity to cultivate their talents, consistent with general social needs. Difficult questions of practice are sure to arise in any functioning social group, but I see no problem of principle.

As for social rewards, it is alleged that in our society remuneration correlates in part with IQ. But insofar as that is true, it is simply a social malady to be overcome much as slavery had to be eliminated at an earlier stage of human history. It is sometimes argued that constructive and creative work will cease unless it leads to material reward, so that all of society gains when the talented receive special rewards. For the mass of the population, then, the message is: "You're better off if you're poor." One can see why this doctrine would appeal to the privileged, but it is difficult to believe that it could be put forth by anyone who has had experience with creative work or workers in the arts, the sciences, crafts, or whatever. The standard arguments for "meritocracy" have no basis in fact or logic, to my knowledge; they rest on a priori beliefs, which, furthermore, do not seem particularly plausible. I have discussed the matter elsewhere and will not pursue it here.[29]

Suppose that inquiry into human nature reveals that human cognitive capacities are highly structured by our genetic program and that there are variations among individuals within a shared framework. This means to me an entirely reasonable expectation, and a situation much to be desired. It has no implications with regard to equality of rights or condition, so far as I can see, beyond those already sketched.

Consider finally the question of race and intellectual endowments. Notice again that in a decent society there would be no social consequences to any discovery that might be made about this question. An individual is what he is; it is only on racist assumptions that he is to be regarded as an instance of his race category, so that social consequences ensue from the discovery that the mean for a certain racial category with respect to some capacity is such-and-such. Eliminating racist assumptions, the facts have no social consequences whatever they may be, and are therefore not worth knowing, from this point of view at least. If there is any purpose to an investigation of the relation between race and some capacity, it must derive from the scientific significance of the question. It is difficult to be precise about questions of scientific merit. Roughly, an inquiry has scientific merit if its results might bear on some general principles of science. One doesn't conduct inquiries into the density of blades of grass on various lawns or innumerable other trivial and pointless questions. Likewise, inquiry into such questions as race and IQ appears to be of virtually no scientific interest. Conceivably, there might be some interest in correlations between partially heritable traits, but if someone were interested in this question he would surely not select such characteristics as race and IQ, each an obscure amalgam of complex properties. Rather, he would

ask whether there is a correlation between measurable and significant traits, say, eye color and length of the big toe. It is difficult
to see how the study of race and IQ can be justified on any scientific grounds.

If the inquiry has no scientific significance and no social significance, apart from the racist assumption that an individual must
be regarded not as what he is but rather as standing at the mean
of his race category, it follows that it has no merit at all. The
question then arises, Why is it pursued with such zeal? Why is it
taken seriously? Attention naturally turns to the racist assumptions
that do confer some importance on the inquiry if they are accepted.

In a racist society, inquiry into race and IQ can be expected to
reinforce prejudice, pretty much independent of the outcome of the
inquiry. Given such concepts as "race" and "IQ," it is to be expected that the results of any inquiry will be obscure and conflicting, the arguments complex and difficult for the layman to
follow. For the racist, the judgment "not proven" will be read
"probably so." There will be ample scope for the racist to wallow
in his prejudices. The very fact that the inquiry is undertaken suggests that its outcome is of some importance, and since it is important only on racist assumptions, these assumptions are insinuated
even when they are not expressed. For such reasons as these, a
scientific investigation of genetic characteristics of Jews would have
been appalling in Nazi Germany. There can be no doubt that the
investigation of race and IQ has been extremely harmful to the
victims of American racism. I have heard black educators describe
in vivid terms the suffering and injury imposed on children who
are made to understand that "science" has demonstrated this or
that about their race, or even finds it necessary to raise the question.

We cannot ignore the fact that we live in a profoundly racist
society, though we like to forget that this is so. When the *New York
Times* editors and U.N. Ambassador Moynihan castigate Idi Amin
of Uganda as a "racist murderer," perhaps correctly, there is a
surge of pride throughout the country and they are lauded for their
courage and honesty. No one would be so vulgar as to observe that
the editors and the Ambassador, in the not very distant past, have
supported racist murder on a scale that exceeds Amin's wildest fan-

tasies. The general failure to be appalled by their hypocritical pronouncements reflects, in the first place, the powerful ideological controls that prevent us from coming to terms with our acts and their significance and, in the second place, the nation's profound commitment to racist principle. The victims of our Asian wars were never regarded as fully human, a fact that can be demonstrated all too easily, to our everlasting shame. As for domestic racism, I need hardly comment.

The scientist, like anyone else, is responsible for the foreseeable consequences of his acts. The point is obvious and generally well understood: consider the conditions on the use of human subjects in experiments. In the present case, an inquiry into race and IQ, regardless of its outcome, will have a severe social cost in a racist society, for the reasons just noted. The scientist who undertakes this inquiry must therefore show that its significance is so great as to outweigh these costs. If, for example, one maintains that this inquiry is justified by the possibility that it may lead to some refinement of social science methodology, as argued by Boston University President John Silber (*Encounter,* August, 1974), he provides an insight into his moral calculus: the possible contribution to research methodology outweighs the social cost of the study of race and IQ in a racist society. Such advocates often seem to believe that they are defending academic freedom, but this is just a muddle. The issue of freedom of research arises here in its conventional form: does the research in question carry costs, and, if so, are they outweighed by its significance? The scientist has no unique right to ignore the likely consequences of what he does.

Once the issue of race and IQ is raised, people who perceive and are concerned by its severe social cost are, in a sense, trapped. They may quite properly dismiss the work on the grounds just sketched. But they do so in a racist society in which, furthermore, people are trained to consign questions of human and social importance to "technical experts," who often prove to be experts in obfuscation and defense of privilege—"experts in legitimation," in Gramsci's phrase. The consequences are obvious. Or, they may enter the arena of argument and counterargument, thus implicitly reinforcing the belief that it makes a difference how the research comes out and tacitly supporting the racist assumptions on which this belief ultimately rests. Inevitably, then, by refuting alleged correlations between race and IQ (or race and X, for any X one selects), one is reinforcing racist assumptions. The dilemma is not restricted to this issue. I have discussed it elsewhere in connection with debate over murder and aggression.[30] In a highly ideological society, matters can hardly be otherwise, a misfortune that we may deplore but cannot easily escape.

We exist and work in given historical conditions. We may try to change them, but cannot ignore them, in the work we undertake, the strategies for social change that we advocate, or the direct action in which we engage or from which we abstain. In discussion of freedom and equality, it is very difficult to disentangle questions of fact from judgments of value. We should try to do so, pursuing factual inquiry where it may lead without dogmatic preconception, but not ignoring the consequences of what we do. We must never forget that what we do is tainted and distorted, inevitably, by the awe of expertise that is induced by social institutions as one device for enforcing passivity and obedience. What we do as scientists, as scholars, as advocates, has consequences, just as our refusal to speak or act has definite consequences. We cannot escape this condition in a society based on concentration of power and privilege. This is a heavy responsibility that the scientist or scholar would not have to bear in a decent society, one in which individuals would not relegate to authorities decisions over their lives or their beliefs. We may and should recommend the simple virtues: honesty and truthfulness, responsibility and concern. But to live by these principles is often no simple matter.

REFERENCES

1. Robert Goodman, *After the Planners* (New York: Simon and Schuster, 1971).

2. K. William Kapp, *The Social Costs of Private Enterprise* (1950; paperback ed., New York: Schocken Books, 1971), p. 231.

3. Cf. Seymour Melman, "Industrial Efficiency under Managerial versus Cooperative Decision-making," *Review of Radical Political Economics,* Spring, 1970; reprinted in B. Horvat, M. Marković, and R. Supek, eds., *Self-Governing Socialism,* vol. II (White Plains, N.Y.: International Arts and

Sciences Press, 1975.) See also Melman, *Decision-Making and Productivity* (Oxford: Blackwell, 1958); and Paul Blumberg, *Industrial Democracy: The Sociology of Participation* (New York: Schocken Books, 1969).

4. Stephen A. Marglin, "What Do Bosses Do?," *Review of Radical Political Economics,* Summer, 1974; Herbert Gintis, "Alienation in Capitalist Society," in R. C. Edwards, M. Reich, and T. E. Weisskopf, eds., *The Capitalist System* (Englewood Cliffs, N.J.: Prentice-Hall, 1972).

5. J. E. Meade, *Efficiency, Equality and the Ownership of Property* (Cambridge: Harvard University Press, 1965).

6. Karl Marx, *Capital,* vol. 3 (Moscow: Foreign Languages Publishing House, 1959).

7. Giambattista Vico, *The New Science,* trans. T. G. Bergin and M. H. Fisch (Garden City, N.J.: Anchor Books, 1961).

8. David Ellerman, "Capitalism and Workers' Self-Management," in G. Hunnius, G. D. Garson, and J. Case, eds., *Workers' Control* (New York: Random House, 1973), pp. 10-11.

9. Adam Smith, *Wealth of Nations,* cited by Marglin, "What Do Bosses Do?"

10. Edward S. Greenberg, "In Defense of Avarice," *Social Policy,* Jan./Feb., 1976, p. 63.

11. "The Fearful Drift of Foreign Policy," Commentary, *Business Week,* Apr. 7, 1975.

12. In fact, in this case, sheer robbery backed by police power is a more likely explanation.

13. On the interpretation of the "lessons of Vietnam" by academic scholars and liberal commentators as the war ended, see my "Remaking of History," *Ramparts,* Sept., 1975, and "The United States and Vietnam," *Vietnam Quarterly,* no. 1, Winter, 1976.

14. For a discussion of this topic, see my introduction to N. Blackstock, *Cointelpro* (New York: Vintage, 1976).

15. See, for example, Herbert J. Gans, "About the Equalitarians," *Columbia Forum,* Spring, 1975.

16. Rudolf Rocker, "Anarchism and Anarcho-Syndicalism," in P. Eltzbacher, ed., *Anarchism* (London: Freedom Press, 1960), pp. 234-35.

17. I have discussed some of the roots of these doctrines elsewhere: e.g., *For Reasons of State* (New York: Pantheon Books, 1973).

18. Rocker, "Anarchism and Anarcho-Syndicalism," p. 228. Rocker is characterizing the "ideology of anarchism." Whether Marx would have welcomed such a conception is a matter of conjecture. As a theoretician of capitalism, he did not have very much to say about the nature of a socialist society. Anarchists, who tended to the view that the workers' organizations must create "not only the ideas but also the facts of the future itself" within capitalist society (Bakunin), correspondingly provided a more extensive theory of post-revolutionary society. For a left-Marxist view of these questions, see Karl Korsch, "On Socialization," in Horvat et al., *Self-Governing Socialism,* vol. 1.

19. Evidently there is a value judgment here, for which I do not apologize.

20. Quotes are from Salvador E. Luria, *Life: The Unfinished Experiment* (New York: Scribner and Sons, 1973).

21. For references and discussion, see note 17, and Frank E. Manual, "In Memoriam: *Critique of the Gotha Program*, 1875-1975," *Daedalus*, Winter, 1976.

22. Fredy Perlman, *Essay on Commodity Fetishism*, reprinted from *Telos*, no. 6 (Somerville, Mass.: New England Free Press, 1968).

23. István Mészáros, *Marx's Theory of Alienation* (London: Merlin Press, 1970).

24. Cited in Mészáros, *Marx's Theory of Alienation*.

25. See my *Reflections on Language* (New York: Pantheon Books, 1975) for reference and discussion.

26. Walter Sullivan, "Scientists Debate Question of Race and Intelligence," *New York Times*, Feb. 23, 1976, p. 23. His account may well be accurate; I have often heard and read similar comments from left-wing scientists.

27. Cf., for example, the remarks on language in Luria, *Life: The Unfinished Experiment;* Jacques Monod, *Chance and Necessity* (New York: Alfred A. Knopf, 1971); François Jacob, *The Logic of Life* (New York: Pantheon Books, 1973). For some recent discussion of this issue, see my *Reflections on Language*.

28. It is extremely misleading to argue, as some do, that certain birds have an elementary "concept of number" as revealed by their ability to employ ordinal and visually presented systems up to some finite limit (about seven). The concepts one, two, . . . , seven are not to be confused with the concept natural number, as formally captured, e.g., by the Dedekind-Peano axioms, and intuitively understood, without difficulty, by normal humans, as an infinite system.

29. See *For Reasons of State*, chap. 7.

30. *American Power and the New Mandarins* (New York: Pantheon Books, 1969), introduction.

Contributors

JAMES D. ANDERSON is assistant professor of educational policy studies at the University of Illinois. He earned his Ph.D. in educational history at the University of Illinois and has taught at Indiana University. He was active in the early stages of the civil rights movement, and his current research involves an analysis of the relationship between industrial interests and black education.

NOAM CHOMSKY is Ferrari P. Ward Professor of Modern Languages at the Massachusetts Institute of Technology. He earned his Ph.D. in linguistics from the University of Pennsylvania and has gained an international reputation for his research in linguistics. *Syntactic Structures, Aspects of the Theory of Syntax,* and *Cartesian Linguistics* are three of his most celebrated works. Professor Chomsky is equally renowned for his analysis of American political, social, and educational policy.

RONALD R. EDMONDS is director of the Center for Urban Studies, Harvard Graduate School of Education, and research associate, Faculty of Education, Harvard Graduate School of Education. He received his M.A. in American history at Eastern Michigan University and has worked and written extensively in the areas of social service reform, black education, and social conflict resolution. One of his recent works is "A Black Response to Christopher Jencks' Inequality."

VIRGINIA HELD is professor of philosophy at City University of New York, Hunter College, and has recently held a Rockefeller Foundation Humanities Fellowship. She earned her Ph.D. at Columbia University and has taught at Barnard College, Columbia University, and Yale University. She writes extensively for academic and popular journals in the fields of ethics and political morality. Among her works are "Moral Responsibility and Collective Action at My Lai 4" and "Marx, Sex, and the Transformation of Society."

JERRY HIRSCH is professor in the department of psychology and the department of ecology, ethology, and evolution at the University of Illinois. He earned his Ph.D. in psychology at the University of California, Berkeley, and has been a fellow at the Center for Advanced Study in the Behavioral Sciences at Stanford. He has held awards from the National Science Foundation and the Social Science Research Council. Professor Hirsch has gained an international reputation for his research in genetics and is best known to the general public for his debates with Arthur Jensen and William Shockley on the heritability of the IQ. He is presently director of a National Institute of Mental Health training program for research on institutional racism.

HU CHANG-TU is professor of education, Teacher's College, Columbia University. A native of China, he earned his Ph.D. in history from the University of Washington. His research and publications have dealt with education in the People's Republic of China.

MIHAILO MARKOVIĆ was recently a senior fellow at the Woodrow Wilson Foundation, Washington, D.C. He was formerly a professor of philosophy at the University of Belgrade and an editor of *PRAXIS*, an eminent Eastern European journal of philosophy. His formal education was completed in Yugoslavia and England. He has written widely on ethics, logic, and political philosophy and is a founder of the KORCULA school of philosophy. He was recognized for his work in the Yugoslavian Resistance during World War II and recently received international attention when he was fired from the University of Belgrade for teachings that were judged contrary to the interests of the state.

WAYNE A. O'NEIL is professor of humanities and linguistics at the Massachusetts Institute of Technology. He earned his Ph.D. in English and Scandinavian linguistics at the University of Wisconsin and has taught at the University of Wisconsin, Duke, and Harvard. He has written extensively in the fields of Scandinavian and English linguistics as well as on American political and educational policy. One of his recent works is "The Language of the Pentagon Papers, or Did They Lie to Each Other, Too?"

ORLANDO PATTERSON is presently a fellow at the Institute for Advanced Study in Princeton. He is on leave from Harvard University where he is a professor of sociology. He has written on such topics as black history and equal opportunity. He serves as an educational consultant to the Prime Minister of Jamaica.